HOW CHILDREN LEARN TO READ

AND HOW TO HELP THEM

Cedric Cullingford

KOGAN
PAGE

First published in 2001

Kogan Page Limited
120 Pentonville Road
London N1 9JN
UK

Stylus Publishing Inc.
22883 Quicksilver Drive
Sterling, VA 20166-2012
USA

British Library Cataloguing in Publication Data

A CIP record for this book is available from the British Library.

ISBN 0 7494 3491 0

Typeset by JS Typesetting, Wellingborough, Northants
Printed and bound in Great Britain by Clays Ltd, St Ives plc

For Anne Gibson

'To be a well-favoured man is the gift of fortune: but to write and read comes by nature'

(Dogberry, *Much Ado about Nothing*, Act III, Scene III)

Motto

'There's glory for you!'

'I don't know what you mean by "glory"', Alice said.

Humpty Dumpty smiled contemptuously. 'Of course you don't till I tell you. I meant "there's a nice knock-down argument for you!"'

'But "glory" doesn't mean "a nice knock-down argument"', Alice objected.

'When I use a word,' Humpty Dumpty said in rather a scornful tone, 'it means just what I choose it to mean – neither more nor less.'

'The question is,' said Alice, 'whether you *can* make words mean so many different thing.'

'The question is,' said Humpty Dumpty, 'which is to be master, that's all.'

(Lewis Carroll, *Through the Looking Glass*, Chapter 6)

Contents

Contents

Preface

The way in which people learn to read has been a fascination for many years. This is partly because learning to read, which seems so simple in hindsight, proves a real difficulty for so many, and partly because the peculiar difficulties of reading, and the strategies needed to overcome them, provide an interesting insight into the nature of learning.

It has also been fascinating to watch initiatives and interventions, theories and methods, come and go over the years. There is little that is new in any of them, and they mostly agree with each other when it comes to practice. Yet the problem remains. So the initiatives, and the arguments that surround them, get fiercer and fiercer and failure to learn to read remains an issue for political blame. Beneath this surface there are all kinds of means that teachers have found help children in their development of reading, and it is on these findings that this book is based.

One of the reasons reading remains a problem is the very way in which it has become subject to constant policy initiatives, each of which implies discredit on what people were doing before. There are, however, different levels to this 'problem'. The first one is the scandal of any form of illiteracy. While we recognize the difficulties peculiar to the English language and its spelling, and the difficulties of personality and circumstance, there is really no excuse for such a significant number of people to have major difficulties with reading. Illiteracy is unnecessary.

A second problem about reading is that much of the attention given to it is devoted to the process of reading rather than the purpose. When people do learn to read this does not imply that their skill is then put to good use. There has always, since the rise of the mass reading public, been a concern that a 'mass' reading public would lead to 'mass' tastes in reading. The learner and the teacher of reading need to be aware that the purpose of reading is the access it gives to understanding. Literacy and numeracy are presented as 'key' skills in the National Curriculum as if they were ends in themselves. They are really a means to a greater end.

Being able to read is an essential for all learning. Hence the panic when standards do not rise. Hence all the new intervention initiatives. Each new programme is seen to work because *any* attempt to help is a good thing. Each new initiative will help on its first introduction, provided it is carried out with conviction. There is just one proviso. For it to last there has to be sympathy for the learner as well as conviction about the method.

Reading can be taught simply, but its learning is complex. Fortunately people have the capacity to pick up clues from different sources. Some have likened learning to read to the playing of a large orchestra, in which many individual instruments make up the whole sound. The individual learner can manage complexity; the enabler needs to focus on the whole.

Given this sympathy, every attempt to help is useful. Without sympathy, intervention comes too late and too mechanically, as if, in Dr Johnson's phrase, the reader were being 'encumbered by help'. The earlier that opportunities to learn to read are given, the better. Many of the processes that enable reading to be learnt seem to have little to do with confrontation with text.

This book depends on years of research carried out by many different people. Many experiments have been written up, many programmes of intervention have been carefully examined and there are many teachers whose skills are aptly documented elsewhere. Rather than encumber this text with a whole apparatus of references, I have chosen to keep them to a minimum. This is meant as an acknowledgement, not a denial, of all the work that has taken place. For those who are interested there are short commentaries on some sources at the end of the book.

Many good teachers are not very good at articulating what they do. In the teaching of grammar, for instance, not all are able to describe all the terms and practices they are so busy demonstrating. The teaching of reading can also be such an almost inarticulate skill. It can be fashionable to deny that learning to read depends on a teacher. There are also many teachers who deny that they were taught how to teach reading. It is too essential, too personal, and too subtle a skill.

Any sympathetic attempt to help can only do good, even if it does so inadvertently. This book is for those who care.

Introduction

Learning to read is an art typical of all learning. It is a process that takes place from birth. It is an ability that enables other forms of learning to take place and it is a skill that can be extended almost infinitely.

Learning to read is not a matter of imbibing information but a means of using information to develop distinct abilities. It is not a skill in the sense of simple manipulation but one that closely involves the complexity of the human mind.

The art of reading exhibits how complex is the process of learning; the translation of ideas into action, the use of actions to create ideas, the recognition of clues, the awareness of context and the realization that clues can be interpreted in a variety of ways. Children need to learn how to read; parents and teachers need to understand the process of learning to enable it to take place, and they need to know how to give the particular clues that make the learning possible.

It is only when children's abilities to learn are understood and fostered that they find it easy to learn to read. Those who help them need to be aware that part of the process of learning is being aware of what can be ignored. Learning is a matter of categorization, a sophisticated choice of significant material. Children's ability to make sense of what they see and hear and translate their perceptions into meaning, and children's use of prediction and guesswork are all part of reading. Children are actively engaged in attempting to understand what reading is for.

Children's attitudes towards reading are therefore very important. The role of parents and teachers in this context is clearly central. The idea of script would be meaningless if it did not convey a story or ideas. It is obvious that spoken language and reading are intimately connected, but it has only comparatively recently been accepted that such a relationship is one of the most important facets of reading. The sense of purpose which reading gives, and the sense that it is a natural and interesting skill, are fundamental to the attitudes that children bring to the curiosities of text.

Knowing the importance of the context in which children learn, and the way in which they learn, makes the role of parents and teachers more, rather than less, important. We need to know how to make use of the environment, and why; how to develop manipulative abilities; how to encourage play, and how to share stories and conversations with children. We also need to know the particular problems of script, many of which are arbitrary rules like the shape of letters, the left to right orientation and the relationship between sounds and signs.

For those who have learnt to read it is sometimes difficult to remember some of the difficulties of the learning process, or some of the anguish for those who are slower than others. The problem is that fluent reading is automatic, internalized. It is no longer a mechanical process. For those who are still aware of individual letters, reading can be a nightmare. The mechanics impede meaning. Rather than look for the clues the temptation is to look away, anywhere, for inspiration.

> Mrs W was terrible. She used to take it out on us. I can remember doing a K, and I used to do my Ks in the infants, and I couldn't do the little Ks and it took me a long time and then when I was trying to learn something the dinner bell would go and I'd get ever so upset at the dinner break because I thought I might get kept in. Once I was trying to read a word and I couldn't find out what this word was and I went to Miss. It was 'the' and because I couldn't read it I was ever so frightened because she kept going on and on and on.
>
> (boy, primary school)

This vignette is unfortunately not unique. Many pupils have felt humiliated by not being able to read. They have been confronted with a demand, or a target, and the more they are cajoled into finding the right answer the more difficult they find it. There is a point when just staring at words, thinking about them, makes them the more peculiar. We have all experienced the phenomenon of looking at unusual spellings. We can get them right with ease, but the more we look at single words the more peculiar they appear. The earlier experiences of reading, unless the clues have been unselfconsciously imbibed, can be matters of confrontation. This 'word blindness' comes about because some kind of clue, some 'secret', appears to be missing. This is not just a matter of knowledge.

We need to be sensitive to the peculiarities of our writing system. Let us take one example. Many words begin with an 'H' (or 'h'). Note that we say 'an' h. The sound 'h' (or 'aitch' as it is called, not as it is pronounced), is recognizable and often a part of a word. And yet it does not exist in itself. Even the most sophisticated of acoustic machines cannot distinguish between the consonant 'h' and the vowels that must follow it. The beginning of the h sound must be followed by some breath. We already have here a hint of the complexity of graphemes, H or h, and phonemes: we know the symbolic sound and meaning of 'h'.

If 'h' does not exist by itself as a sound, it has to be followed, for example by 'a'. Ha. Any reader will know how to pronounce that, as in 'ha-ha', and yet if another letter is added, then that might be a wrong interpretation. 'Hah' remains the same sound, 'hay' changes the sound of the vowels, and so does 'hat', or 'ham'. A logical step-by-step interpretation from left to right does not work. Fluent readers take this for granted. They know that as a word is extended, so its sound needs reinterpreting.

If we therefore read 'hal', we will all pronounce this in the same way, and quite differently from 'ha'. There is only one accepted possibility, unless you add another letter: hale, halt, half. Again, we have three quite different phonemes: recognizable sounds. All this might appear to be pedantic, since we have absorbed these clues and no longer think about them. The clues are, however, crucial to those who are struggling to read. There are systematic ways of reading even meaningless or new words once we know them: 'halm' will be pronounced differently from 'haly'. After a time this distinction becomes routine. Then we can concentrate on what reading means: the power of the word, the pleasure of communication, and the extension of understanding.

The art of learning to read lies not just in the mechanics of the process but in recognizing the pleasures. This realization of the meaning of script must start early. There is no greater advantage than living in a home where reading is observed as a pleasure, both personal and shared. An abundance of books and stories, of dialogue and shared curiosity are more than a head start. This is why what are drily called 'pre-reading skills' are emphasized so strongly.

Some have drawn the analogy between learning to read and learning to ride a bicycle. There is a moment when the idea of balance is no longer theoretical but mastered, and internalized. Learning to read is not as simple as this, although it is a matter of being enabled to learn rather than being told. It needs to be done, in order for it to be understood. This could be argued to be true of all learning. It is a personal matter, which is why some people, rather curiously, resent the idea of being taught. All learning is a matter of context, dependent on other people, on information imbibed as well as on observation and discrimination. Teachers, whether we are aware of it or not, are crucial.

There should be no dichotomy between teaching and learning. There have been times when any difficulties of learning to read were blamed on teachers, and other times when failure was ascribed to stupidity. Difficulties in learning to read, as in dyslexia, arise because of unfamiliarity with either the process of reading or the peculiar learning demands that reading presents, including what to ignore, and how to recognize just the salient clues.

The moment when the secret of reading is suddenly understood, and there often is such a moment, is hard to detect. It is that move from looking at the individual letters to seeing how they form recognizable words. It is seeing how sounds are made up graphically from blends. There are, therefore, certain things, like digraphs, which can be taught.

This book is designed both to explain the process of reading and to translate understanding into action. It combines explanations of how children learn to read and what to do to help them. It uses the experience of teachers and the insight of researchers to suggest ways in which parents and teachers can help children learn.

The book concentrates on different processes of learning to read: those involved with the difficult initial skills and those evoked by the fluent translation of text into meaning, those skills concerned with the sounds of words, and those skills that bypass the process of sounding. For this reason there is a stress on the importance of the uses of literacy, on conveying the ideas behind reading and the abilities needed to interpret the ideas.

Just as the book concentrates on the blending of different kinds of skill and the combining of the context of language with the awareness of how to understand the significant clues, so it concentrates on the particular underlying process of learning to read: the understanding of blends themselves. We know that the understanding of single letters is not enough in itself; the recognition of whole words is not an automatic process without deeper analysis. It is the blending of one sound into another, one letter into another, that lies at the heart of the initial process of learning to read.

The first part of the book gives as short a summary as possible of the way in which children learn and the way in which it affects their ability to read. It also gives an outline of the most significant processes involved in reading. The rest of the book discusses and analyses the development of reading, from pre-reading skills to the more extended processes still being learnt by fluent readers. It does so by giving the means to develop the art of reading, through a large number of practical ideas.

Understanding the ways in which children learn is combined throughout the book with suggestions about the teaching process. Anyone involved in teaching reading should be able to make use of the ideas, and through the ideas think further about the learning of the individual children being taught. Each idea will work differently with different children; each teacher will find his or her own way through. The underlying purpose of the book is to sum up what is known about reading, and to give insight into the ways we can put this knowledge to use. The purpose of the book is, above all, to help.

Part one

How children learn to read

'The books are something like our books, only the words go the wrong way.'

(Lewis Carroll, *Through the Looking Glass*, Chapter 1)

Chapter 1
How children learn

You taught me language, and my profit on't
Is, I know how to curse.

(Shakespeare, *The Tempest*, Act 1 Scene 2)

Caliban's outburst about the ambiguous role of language reveals how ancient and unchanging is the controversy about heredity and environment, between 'nature' and 'nurture', or more recently between 'genetics' and 'environmental determinism'. We all know that we are the products of the circumstances in which we live, sharing the language, culture and attitudes of that part of the world in which we happen to be born. We all accept that we display characteristics that can be traced to our parents, and that these make us distinctive. But to understand how these two forces in us are balanced, and to understand the processes through which we go to become what we are, is a complex matter. Our personalities and attitudes might seem shaped, but our behaviours are our own.

One human characteristic that seems universal is the tendency we have, once we have formed an opinion, to stick to it doggedly even in the face of evidence. Once they have reached a particular point of view, many people concentrate on bolstering their arguments and attacking all alternative opinions. Many of the arguments about the balance between innate intelligence and learned skills are conducted as if there are absolute alternatives. Perhaps there are political motives in suggesting either that children are all born with unchangeable innate abilities, or that they can be formed or moulded in whatever way one wishes. One extreme hypothesis that led to a particular line of research sought to prove that all behaviour is a result of conditioning – that a mixture of rewards and punishments produces particular forms of reaction. Stimuli of any kind, a gesture of approval by a mother, or a bit of food, are assumed to accumulate into a pattern of responses. Against this mode of thought is placed the argument that human beings, unlike animals, are born with innate characteristics that include the ability to use language. Chomsky defined young children's natural abilities with language as if they were 'Language Acquisition Devices'. There is still a tendency for people to polarize these different shaping influences, suggesting for instance that it is all a matter of genetics. Such extreme positions are unhelpful.

The ways in which children come to terms with the world, react to it, form their own perceptions and are formed by what happens to them are a fascinating study for anyone who is as interested in individuals as in general rules. Parents are obviously as excited by the family characteristics their children show, in looks or gesture, as they are by all the signs that children reveal of learning how to respond with their voice or through the manipulation of their hands. The fact of language constantly reminds us of the importance of children's early interactions with others, and the more we learn about very young children, the more it is clear that they are both capable and active in their learning. That children are not mere passive receivers of information is clear; that they are dependent on the circumstances in which they find themselves is equally clear.

Children develop rapidly in the womb, and demonstrate by their reactions that they are already responsive. From the moment they are born, children are actively engaged in trying to make sense of the sounds and sights of the world, and are therefore, in a sense, already beginning the first stage of learning to read. Newborn infants constantly explore what they see in a systematic way. They are trying to understand what they see and hear by finding some characteristic consistency or pattern. They are seeking meaning. The first task of learning is to understand how to focus on, and recognize, relevant clues. At first the world looks like a mass of colours and shapes; parts of which move and parts of which are still, parts of which are light and parts of which are dark. By the gradual accumulation of small clues, and by many perceptual guesses, the complex disarray of visual impressions is understood through the recognition of constituent parts as a coherent whole. Faces become familiar, primary colours stand out, objects are perceived to be close or farther away. Learning to discriminate starts from the beginning. Gradually children make sense of what they have learnt, at first in their own way and then in ways that are closer to the conventions with which adults view the world.

Most of us take for granted many of the clues that children are still exploring. We automatically concentrate on sounds that are significant to us, and ignore others, responding to a voice and blocking off the music in the background. Children need to learn to focus on *one* item of information seen or heard rather than another. While ostensibly attending to a voice they can be more aware of other sounds that are going on: the sound of the wind, the sound of an aircraft, the buzzing of a fly on the windowpane or the bustle of other children. True listening means taking in all these sounds; but conventional attention demands that just one significant source of sound is attended to at any one time.

Learning is a matter of predicting and guessing which perceptions are significant and which are not. It can be a painful struggle for babies and toddlers to know what they are supposed to see and understand. Without any particular starting point, they often flounder through a series of guesses based on their own version of events. But this difficulty can remain for older children. Perhaps the best illustration of this is the way in which children do not take in implied rules, or unspoken assumptions. When a teacher says 'Go and shut the door', she usually means 'Get up quietly and without disturbing anyone else'. For children every act is far richer than the more mechanical actions of adults. An adult going to close the door will march straight across the room. A child will tend to stop on the way, look out of the window, nudge someone else, try a different way of walking. This is not daydreaming but an indication of a way of seeing the world that has not become completely focused on a task in hand. For adults it is usually clear what convention demands, which clues, perceptual or cultural, need to be ignored and which rules are implied. For children the task of learning is not only a matter of prediction or guessing but also a matter of learning what to ignore and how to focus on the particular.

Children's idiosyncratic view of the world is a result of this constant engagement in learning rules, whether of perception or behaviour or reading. Their interest in fairy stories is part of this engagement in trying to make personal sense of the world they are in. They know consistencies are important but do not always know what these are. Some of the worst traumas of childhood come about because the rules that children think are being applied are suddenly changed, or an excitement in which they are caught up is suddenly broken from outside. The cry from the heart that characterizes children's deepest dissatisfaction is that 'it's not fair'. Suddenly their own consistent sense of the world and its patterning is broken by a change in convention.

11

Children's involvement in their learning, shown by their curiosity and capacity to go on being curious, means that they are constantly refining their point of view against others. Children are not empty vessels slowly being filled up with more information, or creatures incapable of rational thought. They have a picture of the world that is wholly their own, and which to adults seems merely idiosyncratic. Their picture of the world has its own rules including a clear distinction between good and bad. Children understand in their own way; they explore and play with ideas actively. Even the mistakes they make show their desire for inner consistency. Even their attempts to emulate the world as they see it are more of a parody than an imitation.

Such a display of mental activity needs a variety of stimulation against which to develop. Parents clearly play a critical part. Without their parents' alert responsiveness and ability to sustain a dialogue, children do not gain the necessary ability to analyse the world in which they find themselves. The desire to learn is innate, so deep-seated as to be taken for granted; but this desire needs to be encouraged. Even deaf children, for example, display the same range of sounds that other children try out, but for lack of any audible response they become silent. Lack of answers, of any kind, in sound or touch or gesture, gradually creates a world in which a child feels him- or herself to be separate. Children start by being capable of a close, optimistic relationship with the world about them; it is the lack of close attention that makes them become enveloped in a world that is entirely their own.

Parents, therefore, are the first and most important teachers. Children test out their voices and ears in their versions of conversation, listen to the different sounds which, like lullabies, contain distinct meanings and effects. Children parody the sounds of language that they hear in what is called 'babbling', and gradually become attuned to the distinctive sounds of the language around them. Parents are not only engaged in supplying warmth, food and comfort but in supplying dialogue and explanations through which children learn to perceive the meaning and structure in the world. In supplying toys, parents are also giving children their first learning tools to help them order and manipulate their surroundings.

From the beginning children are engaged in mental as well as perceptual activity. Indeed, it is hard to separate the two. The cerebral activity that is a common denominator of all learning is the need to categorize, to make distinctions and to generalize from experience. The greatest feat of learning is to know what makes one event distinct, and how to perceive the rule that makes it applicable elsewhere. It has been suggested that all learning is a matter of being able to draw up categories; to see the uniqueness of every dog, on the one hand, and see that the term 'dog' applies to creatures of all kinds of size and shape, from poodles to Saint Bernards, on the other. For young children the ability to recognize the same face, and the ability to recognize faces as a distinct phenomenon, and then the ability to understand that within each individual and uniquely different visage, a smile means something special, is just one of many examples of this development of under- standing.

The power of children's early learning is not always recognized because it is difficult to relate it simply to the terms in which adult cognitive development would be discussed. There tends to be an assumption that children are rather limited, and that it is only when they are capable of mental acts at a particular stage that they can be said to 'think' in the normal sense of the term. But it is clear that such a view of children's limitations is based on a very careful choice of what should be tested, and through a very particular and very limited use of linguistic experiment. The fact that it is difficult to test children's recall until they have the language in which to explain it has led to the assumption that children are not capable of recall. They might not have the capacity to explain what they are learning, but are nevertheless applying this capacity to the learning of language.

The rapidity with which children learn language is itself remarkable, especially when it is considered that most of what they learn is through their sense of context. Every extension of their vocabulary comes about through some form of guesswork and through actual use. Every new word in a conversation or in a book gradually has its own characteristic meaning defined by the use in a variety of different contexts. The richer in language their environment, the better chance children have to develop. The fact that not all do so shows up the important distinction between what children are capable of learning, or expressing, and what children actually do learn.

This distinction between capacity and performance is one that remains with people throughout their lives, for no one is mentally alert all the time. It is tempting to view learning as a constantly increasing cognitive mastery: but if this were so, all teaching would be simply a matter of conveying information. There are no distinct stages through which all children go at a particular age; nor is there a steady curve of cognitive improvement. Instead, since the ability to learn depends so much on seeing the relationship between different things, there are moments when children suddenly seem to have learnt a great deal and others when they seem to be at a standstill. Learning is not so much a matter of steady accumulation as a matter of adaptation. Each year might bring particular characteristics to children, and there are certain changes that children might go through. But the more we learn about different kinds of learning, the more we see that adults, like children, 'regress' to states of inarticulacy, of less than perfect rationality. Before we make a distinction between 'childishness' and 'inactivity' it is worth reminding ourselves that varying states of consciousness in adults are just as ambiguous as in children, if usually better disguised.

Not all children learn at the same rate; nor do all children learn in the same way. Some children approach the task of ordering the material that confronts them in a systematic way; others wait until they can see the whole solution at once. Children learn as much through their powers of imaging as through their powers of logic. Children learn through associations just as they learn through the amount of attention they bring to bear. Many of the subconscious attitudes, expectations and associations are as important to children's learning as their ability to gain cerebral mastery over the organization of facts.

Accepting that children learn rapidly in their own way and have a strong desire to do so should help parents and teachers understand how they can assist and give them the means to develop. They will understand why children find what seem like simple tasks so difficult; why, when confronted by a word they can't read, children will look away, out of the window, at their friends for comfort, at anything but the task in hand. Understanding that learning is an active process also helps us create the means by which children can help themselves. For the process of learning, and the mastery of language, underlies the task of reading. Reading can be taken as a symbol of learning; it encapsulates the need to predict, to understand categories, to see which clues make sense and which do not, to see the purpose behind the text and not to be put off by the seeming arbitrariness of some of the rules. Reading gives an insight into the world without which a child will be powerless. As Humpty Dumpty said, 'It depends who is to be master'.

Chapter 2
The process of learning to read

Children learn to read from the moment that they make sense of language, for reading brings together the abilities of visual and auditory discrimination that children explore from birth, and the sense of meaning that language engenders. Any form of learning combines a variety of skills, abilities and definitions; the learning of language, in which reading is subsumed, is more complex than most. But because reading is a task so vital to so many others, and because it is so central to what takes place in schools, there have been many attempts to reduce the sense of complexity into a simple process, by means of teaching strategies that do not take into account all we know about the power of the mind to discriminate and to retain information. It is important to place the learning of reading in the wider context of learning, and recognize that it is more than a battleground between different approaches to the teaching of skills. This recognition of the importance of understanding the process of learning to read is both hopeful and liberating; it shows how important is the role of the parent as well as the teacher, and accepts that there are many things that can be done to help, most of which are not very technical or complicated.

Some of the complexities that apply to reading have already been met, and overcome, in the learning of language. Even the ability to make sense of listening is a process of precise analysis and prediction as well as response. Every person speaks in a different way: he or she has his or her own 'ideolect'. Each person's voice is unique and can be shown to be so when analysed on a tape. And yet we can all understand each other, because the sounds we make correspond nearly enough to the sounds, the phonemes, that other people make. We become used to different accents and different dialects, pronouncing 'book', for example, according to whether we are in the north or south, and yet this is no barrier to recognition. Children have to learn which sounds are meaningful entities, or phonemes. When a child first makes noises they have little bearing on speech; gradually every child learns to copy the sounds that carry recognizable meanings. Parents tend to talk to their infants of around three months old as if everything can be understood, but when the child starts to respond verbally, they simplify what they say, and develop a kind of 'baby talk'. This reveals that they instinctively recognize that children are learning the sound rules of the language, particularly sounds that recognizably belong to a particular language.

Every language has a different set of phonemes. In English 'l' is one phoneme, although we know that it has two different sounds, when we notice where our tongue rests when we say 'fee*l*' or '*l*eaf'. In other languages such a difference generates two different phonemes. In Arabic the 'p's in 's*p*in' and '*p*in' are different. In Chinese there is no phonemic distinction between the two English phonemes 'l' and 'r'. Each language uses different segments of sound to carry distinct meanings. Children need to learn that out of all the varieties of sound, only a number convey meanings. They need to learn which clues to acknowledge, and which sounds to ignore. It might be acceptable, if excruciating for some, to rhyme poem, home and gnome. We would know that at least the last two are supposed to rhyme. For young children, all three words are equally distinct from each other, just as each voice is distinct. They have to learn phoneme conventions.

While children try to make sense of our linguistic system they are constantly guessing what the rules are supposed to be. Their ability to see that there is a series of rules is such that many of their own mistakes are based on their understanding of these rules. When children make mistakes of syntax they often do so because they have transferred a rule, like 'ed' as in 'banged', signifying the past tense, to words that do not follow the logical rules: 'He hitted me'. The language that we use both sets up conventions and breaks them; and one of the difficulties for children is to know when rules are important and when they are not.

Sometimes the difficulties come about because the surface difficulties get in the way of underlying meanings. This can be shown by the difference between the 'deep' and 'surface' structures of three sentences that look the same but carry quite different meanings.

They are buying glasses.
They are drinking glasses.
They are drinking companions.

People have an innate sense of grammar or structure, based on mean-ing. This is developed through understanding the context in which new meanings are embedded. Children's ability to think through the implications of what they are learning takes place at a deeper level than is easily noticed. They not only see the sense of the unit of meaning (morpheme) '-ed', and apply it to other words, but also first learn to apply it to those words denoting activities that can come to an end, like 'dropped, jumped, closed'. They then learn to apply 'ed' to words denoting activities that you can go on doing: 'talked, walked, watched'. And all this is learnt through an understanding of the context in which these sounds are used. Stories reveal new words together with clues as to what they might mean.

Without a firm grounding in the use of language children will not be able to make much sense of reading. If the learning of reading is seen as a separate activity from the conveying of meaning it loses its sense of purpose. Children can be prepared for the ability to read from the start; the more active the encouragement to use words, to make discriminations of sound and sight, and to understand categories, the easier will be the development of reading. For this reason the term 'reading readiness', when applied to a stage at which children are suddenly prepared, is not very helpful. Obviously there are certain abilities that must be fostered before the text is presented to a child. There are times when the child has not been prepared for the initial stages of reading and is merely alarmed by a sudden confrontation with a meaningless task. The preparation for reading is such an active process that it is impossible to chose a particular time when children are supposed to be reading. Each child develops in an idiosyncratic way; some are early to talk or to crawl, and learn to read naturally at the age of three. Others learn to understand the point of reading much later. There is an apocryphal story about George Bernard Shaw who never said a word, let alone read a word, until the age of seven when he complained about the porridge. When his parents, delighted to hear him talk at last, asked why he had not done so before, he replied, 'Until now the service has been perfectly satisfactory'.

The development of children's language flows naturally into their understanding of reading. There are many sub-skills involved in reading: understanding the ways in which dimensions work, or the concept of a one-way flow from left to right. Children can acquire a thorough grounding in all aspects of visual discrimination before they are confronted with a script or a series of letters. Such preparation can take place at almost any time. Children learn in certain sequences, but they do not need sequences imposed upon them.

One of the most important aspects in the process of learning to read is children's attitude to reading. If children understand what reading is for they have made a great start; if they wish to learn to read because they realize that it is the means of enjoying stories, they will have less difficulty in translating desire into performance. A home in which books are a normal part of daily activity, and parents who share picture books and stories with their children, are the perfect conditions in which children learn to read. The shared activity of looking at a book, turning over the pages, following the story from left to right, and the ability to test the accuracy of the reader against the memory of the script, all make up the realization that there is an underlying purpose in reading. We often find children parodying the act of reading. Pretending to read is a good preparation for the real thing.

In all the summaries of research on reading it is clear that the role of parents is crucial, not only in the early stages but later. There are four underlying needs that make it possible for children to learn to read: an environment rich in language, attachment to adults who read a lot themselves, the ability to discriminate and categorize, and interaction with adults interested in teaching children to read. Children pick up the attitudes of those around them, and can be put off reading as easily as they can be encouraged to develop it. Even the well-meaning can make it difficult for children to learn, for an association of reading with particular learning styles or tasks can make them stubbornly backward. In primary schools it is often found that children consistently discriminate between valuing reading and enjoying it. If this distinction is too finely drawn, children have difficulties in understanding even the psychomotor skills that go into reading. They react against the whole idea of reading. A complex task at school, forced on children in the wrong way, can make them turn all their mental attention away from the task to different styles of avoidance. Many children develop mixed attitudes towards reading; enjoying it at home but associating it with the necessities of school. Once reading is seen as a barrier to learning it is much more difficult to help children. For this reason the help that parents give and the attitudes they present are of great importance.

Children need to be encouraged to accept reading as a natural task. If there is a close connection between the development of language and reading, then the peculiarities of our system of spelling should not be an impediment. Once the connection is lost, however, writing appears to be nothing but a jumble of meaningless marks. It is unfortunately rather easy to present reading as a series of arcane hieroglyphics. Some of the 'stories' designed to help children learn to read can be very dull because of the lack of meaning, and are sometimes an insult to the mental level of children. Reading schemes based purely on phonic principles – 'I can fan a sad man, I can fan a tan man, can I fan a mad man' – are not only meaningless but are actually difficult for adults to read. The reason mechanistic approaches to reading are so virulently attacked is that they demean the art of reading for meaning. Children are capable of very difficult achievements. Chinese children, for example, learn to read very complex orthographies very rapidly. When children make mistakes, it is argued, these come about because they have a strong sense of meaning, which they are trying to match to the words on the page. Children's difficulties, in fact, come from knowing too much, rather than too little.

One of the most fruitful means of gaining insight into the process of learning to read has come about from the analysis of the mistakes that children make. Just as they make mistakes in syntax through the contrast between their sense of rules and structure, and the irregularity of the words that confront them, so children apply their inner sense of meaning to the words on a page. When they misread, this is often the result of a subconscious need to respond to an idea having little to do with the actual printed page.

Mistakes should not be a matter of scorn, but seen as signs of the complexity of learning; the relationship between the inner need to make sense of the world, and the need to guess which clues, out of a whole range of stimuli, are those that signal conventional meanings. Very few of the mistakes that children make contain no sense at all; it is suggested that over 86 per cent of substitutions make sense better than, or at least are equal to, the original text. For such analysts every mistake a child makes has a reason, with its roots in the subconscious.

One of the most influential analysers, Goodman, viewed reading as a 'psycholinguistic guessing game'. Research into the mistakes that children make shows how they search for particular clues, rather as a deaf person, having lip-read enough clues to see what people are likely to be saying, becomes comparatively fluent until the subject suddenly changes. Readers often guess or predict what is there and anticipate what will come next.

The guesses that take place in reading are not random if children are concentrating. They are attempts to pursue meanings, to connect the peculiarities of script with the sense of language. Once some of the minimal clues are understood, they are then applied to other passages, sometimes with success that confirms the children's understanding and sometimes with a mismatch.

The concept of intelligent guessing, or of trying to match predictions with ever increasing certainty, suggests that reading is more a matter of knowing what to look for than of knowing how to look. All aspects of reading involve the reduction of uncertainty. 'Whole words' or the recognition of particular letters depends on categories and understood features. The reader needs to know two sources of information: the visual and the sequential, which is the knowledge of the way words are constructed.

If children are helped to develop their own abilities, and have the confidence to see the task of reading as one that does not imply a great barrier, the particular difficulties of reading can be overcome more easily. But reading is not just a matter of guesswork, or the application of language to a new means of communication. Reading presents certain problems because it is a code that needs to be learnt, not only through memory but through the knowledge of which clues are consistent and which are not. Reading subsumes the archetypal forms of learning in a particular way. It includes the need to be able to develop memory. It depends upon children's ability to categorize. It relies on the fact that children are actively involved in learning, for no one learns to read through the passive reception of information. At the same time reading causes difficulties because, unlike language, it has no meaning in itself, but is a process used for the sake of something else. Children's development of speech depends on meaning rather than on structure. Children possess innate cognitive capacities rather than innate syntactic rules. These capabilities determine how they create their own categories of reality. While children are continuously making their own sense of the world, it is the learning of reading that for some of them is the particular skill that causes so much difficulty, since the clues are at once so arbitrary and so limited. For some children, the more of their semantic capacity they bring to bear, the more difficult is the task of reading.

The mistakes children make in reading reveal the way in which they follow clues as far as they can, even if it leads to mistakes. They go down the 'wrong garden path', guessing what will come next, computing only one reading until they are suddenly surprised, just as one is when discovering that the following sentence is not, ultimately, ambiguous: 'I was afraid of Lewis's powerful punch, especially as it had already laid out many tougher men who had bragged they could handle that much alcohol.'

It is understandable that one interprets a sentence while reading it; one does not wait until the end before one applies the mind. The most telling clues in language are those of context, the place in the story in which a word is first met, just as the interpretation of many words depends on the circumstances in which they are uttered as well as the tone in which they are uttered. Children look for and need clues that fit their own experience.

Children's ability to develop language is a very important part of the process of reading, but it has already been indicated that reading does not wholly depend on their linguistic ability. The problem with learning to read is that it consists of two processes taking place at the same time. It is clear that a fluent reader can extract significant clues very fast. Much of what takes place, despite the way that the eye jumps, and fixates, or perhaps because of these saccadic movements, is a matter of perceptual guesswork, looking for clues. Skilled readers recognize the meanings of more words than are fixated, and use those words as markers to guide their eyes to the location of the next useful fixation. The ability to be led by the meaning of a text is shown in the way in which fluent readers combine visual and context clues, and in their storing of semantic information. Fluent readers evolve a distinct style of reading. Beginning readers look at just one element at a time.

The reading process consists of two distinct styles, which might be termed 'word identification' and 'reading for comprehension', or 'learning to read' and 'fluent reading'. The earliest stages of reading combine the two, so that beginners have to learn special skills that will be of no use to them later. Some words they recognize at once, like fluent readers. Other words they need to analyse into each constituent part. No amount of hope, or knowledge of distinctive features completely overcomes the need to understand the code that makes up the blending of letters into words. This complex mixture of meaning and the composition of letters has long been recognized, but not understood in such a way as to help the teaching of reading, mainly because most techniques have concentrated *either* on words *or* on letters, whereas the process of learning to read consists of both understanding and the analysis of significant clues.

The combination of the two processes of learning to read is so complex that 'meaning' can sometimes actually get in the way of decoding. It was found that five-year-olds who could read:

Go back must word you your on not

could not read:

You must not go back on your word.

For adults it is, of course, the other way round. The first sentence is far more difficult to read, and slower. Early readers take one word at a time as if each entity had only a meaning specific to itself. And yet, at the same time, they are fluent with spoken language.

One of the most important distinctions in learning is that between 'knowing that' and 'knowing how', a distinction both powerful and deep-rooted. One type of learning is to acquire definite skills, like drawing an animal; another is modification of behaviour as a result of events and experience. The process of learning to read involves both. We must underline the importance of experience, the sense of meaning and the centrality of attitudes towards reading. There have been two distinct traditions in the theory of reading: the 'linear', with its picture of readers decoding letters serially and systematically decoding them into phonemes, and the 'integrated', in which the higher and lower-order processes of learning are integrated into a 'psycholinguistic guessing game'.

The proper understanding of the teaching of reading needs to be based on the combination of both models. The difference between the skilled and unskilled reader lies in the fact that the former can do with less information. Eye movements are guided by overall textual structure but also by the reader's task. All the explanations of the process of reading need to combine different elements. It is important to recognize that a child's experience is an essential element, that attitudes engendered by parents are crucial, and that it is possible, through games, talk and stories, as well as the encouragement of perceptual discrimination, to help a child learn to read from a very early age. Placing the learning of reading within its larger context not only avoids some of the aridity of traditional teaching methods, but gives impetus to the pleasure that parents and teachers share in observing children's great, if idiosyncratic, ability to learn.

Chapter 3
The skills of learning to read

The problem with learning to read can be expressed quite simply:

ㄌ ㄈㄥㄨ ㄑ ㄥ ㄓ ㄚ ㄕ ㄩ

We are confronted with this series of marks, and have the advantage of understanding that we are to translate the written symbols into sounds. How do we go about it? Given our experience of reading, do we know how to begin to decode the marks? Must we first decide whether this is a series of words or a series of letters, one word or one sentence? Does it run from right to left? Do the symbols have any equivalent in sound, or are we contemplating a script like Chinese that is based on ideograms? Of course we will never be able to read these symbols, for we cannot answer those basic questions without much more information.

The idea of what reading is for is as important a basis as the development of language, but it is not enough in itself. To understand the marks we would need to know something about the way the system works and what the symbols represent. When children learn to develop their understanding of reading, they are also learning a sense of distinct skills, skills that apply only to our language. We read English from left to right (unlike Arabic), and we read through a correlation of symbols to sounds (unlike the Chinese). Each written language consists of a series of agreed codes. Think of someone approaching the following symbols for the first time:

C O N C E N T R A T E

This is as difficult an experience as the first hieroglyphics.

Children can very easily put up barriers against learning if they are bewildered by the gap between the insistence that they should react to a series of signs, and the lack of any clues as to how they should react. When children have difficulties with reading it is because some of the essential rules have not been made clear. Unlike speaking, learning to read is not a 'natural' ability. The way in which our language is written is fairly complex and sometimes arbitrary. We depend on a series of accepted correspondences that are not always exact. We accept a series of conventions within which we can distinguish one script from another. For children the difficult stages of learning to read are those in which they understand that there are clues that others take for granted but that they cannot see. Reading can seem like a closed world that others know about and they cannot enter.

Children are being prepared to enter the world of reading while they listen to stories, see books and understand that meanings depend upon focusing attention on particular clues.

Ǝ T A R T N Ǝ Ɔ N O Ɔ

Gradually they begin to be slightly more familiar with the 'tactics' of scripts. The idea of sight/sound correspondence is something subconsciously imbibed. They realize that they need to concentrate upon interpreting two dimensions rather than three; and that letter shapes only make sense when looked at from *one* direction. Thus a red toy car remains a red toy car whether it is being held upside down or not; but the letter 'p' changes its meaning when it is seen from upside down. Thus gradually children learn some of the underlying but essential skills of reading until they are not only familiar with the problem, but can see means of tackling it.

E T A R T N E C N O C

When children learn to read they understand the purpose of putting sounds on paper, and they recognize the particular ways in which this can be done. They have to understand what is arbitrary and what is constant. Just as they develop their own rules to make the complex world coherent in their minds, and just as their syntactical mistakes are often based on reason, so the mistakes they make in reading come about from the difficulties of knowing which clues are consistent and which are changeable. 'M', for example, stands for the same sound all the time, 'g' stands for the sound as in 'get' 69 per cent of the time, and vowels keep putting on different disguises, according to the context in which they are found. When children make spelling mistakes they do so with a certain consistency. Pre-school children might write out 'Fish swimming in water' as:

FES SOWEMEG EN WOODR

but even this is written with some purpose rather than with random symbols. Their mistakes might seem independent from adult systems, but they already see the underlying point of the alphabet and sound equivalents. In writing, children slowly try to create enough clues to reinterpret what they have written. This is rather like the fluent reader also looking for enough clues to make sense of what he or she sees.

If y are a flt reodur y will have no diflucky readg this.

For young children as well as for fluent readers, the need is to search for enough meanings to make sense of what is seen, but the impediments to doing this differ.

Although early and developed styles of reading have a great deal in common, they are also in contrast to each other. The young child is desperately trying to work out all the clues, and failing to find them; the fluent reader, knowing all the clues, chooses to ignore them. The differences between word identification and reading for comprehension remain. When fluent readers meet a new word they also revert to a less familiar style of interpretation. Even young children attempt to reconcile the two processes of reading: that of understanding the idea, the seeking of meaning, and that of understanding the techniques involved. Once children see the peculiar requirements of written script they can suddenly transpose their knowledge to other circumstances. This essential discovery of learning how script works can be best likened to being confronted with a French poem:

Un petit d'un petit
S'étonne aux Halles,
Un petit d'un petit
Ah! degrés te fallent.

However good our French, this little extract is not going to seem of any particular significance. But once we are told that it is a version of Humpty Dumpty with a French accent, the whole idea is transformed. Once the clue is recognized the rest follows almost inevitably.

The problem for children is that most clues to learning to read are not that simple. At one level, understanding the concept of reading does depend on such a clue, but on another it is more a matter of subtle and changing interpretations. The fact that we make use of 44 distinct sounds that carry meaning (phonemes), while using only 26 letters, itself creates difficulties. A letter can mean a large number of different sounds. 'A' as in 'all' is in contrast to 'a' as in 'any', 'want', 'at', or 'calm'. At the same time we are able to write out the same sound in a variety of different spellings. If we take the sound 'i' as in 'child' we find it appears in a number of disguises: 'aisle', 'height', 'lie', 'sign', 'high', 'island', 'guide', 'buy', 'dye', 'by' . . . and so on. As if this were not enough, we are able to write the same letter in a number of different ways even in print, let alone in the idiosyncrasies of handwriting. Each typescript is different: A, a, *a*, etc.

The Bullock Report made famous particular examples of the problem of orthography. The word 'ghoti' will not mean much in English but it is a way of spelling the word 'fish' if we combine 'gh' is in 'rough'; 'o' as in 'woman' and 'ti' as in 'nation'. 'Calmbost' is an alternative way of using similar sounds to spell 'chemist'. It is very easy to give examples of the eccentricities of spelling. They point up the particular difficulties children have with rules that are never completely certain. In fact, as we will see, the orthographic system is not that much of a problem, but it does underline the ways in which it can be difficult for children to understand the simplest techniques, since reading is partly a matter of reducing uncertainty. The difficulties for children are those not merely of seeing how rules work, but of understanding that rules are rather shifty. Once the idea of rules is grasped, however, the difficulties are a comparatively minor problem. They become a major problem if the child has not yet learnt enough of the basic skills to understand anything but the unfairness of eccentric associations between hieroglyphics and sounds.

It is possible to overcome some of the problems of early reading only if they are seen in the larger context of language. To ignore the problems of orthography is pointless; but solving the problems is not an end in itself. Reading is so rooted in the rules of language that many of the supposed difficulties arise out of semantics. Readers are so accustomed to expect certain things that they look for those clues that are closest to spoken language. The constraints of phonology are such that even speech errors are of a certain kind; slips of the tongue will almost always be of the same order; 'Stips of the lung' rather than 'Tlips of the sung'. When readers go through a passage of prose to search out all the 'e's, they can see that they often miss many that are silent in speech – such as in 'mile' – but not those that are sounded, such as in 'meat'. In fact readers are so accustomed to the expected and to the relationship of words to meanings that it is very uncomfortable to read the following:

When they herd bear feat in the haul the buoy tolled hymn he had scene a none.

Reading is always approached with an important set of prior consider-ations. The way that a passage is tackled depends not only on the nature of the content and its style, but on the purpose with which it is read. There is always a complex relationship between the style of reading and the style of the material, and never more complex than in young children's first approaches. Children are deeply absorbed in their own styles, even if they are ostensibly concerned with the nature of the passage they are supposed to read. The barrier they face can be that of processing particular words, or that of the meaning and purpose of the task, or both. The capacity of children to absorb information is far greater than the level of performance being demanded by the task of reading. If there is an expectation of success and an acknowledgement of the difficulty, and a realization of how our coding works, then many of the complexities of the skills involved are more easily overcome.

We should remember that reading does not consist of remembering; as subtle as the connection between language and thought, reading is an ability to translate symbol into meaning through sound, a use of sound that the fluent reader almost entirely ignores, as in speed reading. The capacity of children to learn is often illustrated by the example of Chinese children who learn to read complex orthography rapidly. The simplification of Chinese characters in 1958 consisted of a reduction from 544 characters with an average of 16.08 strokes to 515 characters with an average of 8.16 strokes. The task remains enormous, but it is, in a sense, one of a different kind of complexity than that of European languages. The idea of a symbol, a picture conveying meaning, is different from the idea of a symbol conveying sounds, and meaning through the sounds. What the experience of Japanese, Chinese and Jewish children reveals is that complex orthography is not in itself the major problem in reading.

Too much has sometimes been made of the complexities of English spellings. The problems are not so acute when compared to the consist-encies. The problem lies in creating an attitude or a condition in which reading is desired, and an understanding of the essential mechanics through which reading is achieved. Most children will perceive the nature of the task through observation; some children will need to be helped to realize what to look for. The eccentricities of the script, as we can see with adult readers,

az wee kan c wit odilt wleagers

are a slight problem compared to the task of knowing how to see meaning in context. Young children make systematic attempts to internalize the rules of the spelling system so that they can quickly understand the likely nature of a word. The visual clues, taken with contextual clues, are bases for them to make sense of script. There is a natural desire for them to guess real words; their mistakes are hardly ever those of creating meaningless words. The important skills, therefore, are not those of knowing every exception to the rules, but knowing the rules, not the rules of spelling, but the distinctive features of reading. Children need to internalize the skills so that the skills themselves do not become a barrier. For this reason many of the pre-reading skills are a form of preparation for later tasks, in terms of discrimination, categorization and context. Once simple tasks are fluent then the desire to make sense of script will help children learn rapidly. Nothing is more important than children's desire to read, and our creating the conditions for this desire. But one of the best ways of fostering the desire to read is to show the rewards that come with it.

Chapter 4
Impediments to learning to read

All things being equal, everyone should learn to read early and easily and with great pleasure. All things are not equal, and there are many for whom learning to read becomes a barrier, both to their intellectual development and their self-esteem. There are difficulties in learning to read, both psychological and academic, which this book explores, and which can be overcome. But there are other external influences that can do a great deal of harm. It is important to be aware of these.

The pleasure of being able to read fluently is taken for granted. The satisfaction of what is read, whether erudite information or great literature, is not. Reading is merely the process through which one has access to the empowerment of the text. The lack of this ability draws attention to the crucial impediment, the inability to enter a world that draws all other people together. The first impediment, therefore, is the very importance of the skill. It is something that *has* to be learnt, that appears to be simple for everyone else – like telling the time – and which seems the more difficult and the more mysterious the more other people make use of it with such equanimity.

This crucial difficulty is fostered, though not deliberately, by the way in which it is treated. Reading is essential. All other learning is, to a large extent, dependent on it. The pressure on the pupil to do well is not only intense, but applied in various ways by others around him or her. Because reading is seen as vital, and because there is a sense that it is a scandal that so many people are to some extent illiterate, it is often under public scrutiny. This has two results. Those who are involved in the teaching of reading are put under more pressure, and the means to put the matter right, as a matter of policy, are the more urgently sought.

The inadvertent pressure on those involved with teaching is unfort-unate. Pupils detect this. They are aware that it matters to teachers and others that they do well. They interpret this not as a sign that teachers care for them, but as a sign that teachers are protective, under inspection, of their own jobs and status. Having one child in a class who holds the others back, or who demands singular attention and is distracting, is bad enough. Being then at least potentially berated for poor standards merely compounds the difficulty.

The tendency to blame, to single out parents, teachers and schools for failing to meet set targets, has the opposite effects to those intended. Just as the pupil suffers from the intensity of psychological expectation, leading him or her to turn away, to escape from the task, so the constants risk of blame and its attendant humiliation makes the position of the teacher very difficult. Why there should be such relish in blaming teachers is an interesting socio-cultural puzzle, but it is an important factor. The blame, of course, is a collective one, not personally directed at individuals. But it is taken personally, as if the 'failure' of the pupil could only be ascribed to an individual: the pupil him- or herself, the teacher, or the parent.

Could one impediment be something greater, like the system, or the techniques, or the policies? There is an irony here. The more the concern with the teaching of reading, the more tempting is the tendency towards policy hysteria. Other major impediments to the learning of reading are the number and weight of policy initiatives. There are many intervention programmes. Each of them means well, and is proved to do well, if implemented with conviction. And yet . . .

Children are very sensitive to moods. They can detect the changes in tone of their parents and their teachers. Indeed they can be almost over-sensitive to perceived feelings and to potential antipathies and impatience. This awareness is not confined to the immediate and the personal, nor to those who have a sense of ontological insecurity. The tones of expectation and disappointment are easily detected. At the same time, children are aware of news. They see hours of television, and while they might prefer those programmes aimed entirely at entertainment they are not unaware of the news, of the kinds of general conversation that are publicly shared. They are therefore aware of the undercurrent of debate about reading standards and the air of scandal that surrounds it. They know they are personally involved and feel responsible to those who are causing the political blame and the personal anxieties of teachers.

At both a personal and a general level, those involved with attempt-ing to overcome the failures to read feel the weight of the political debate. It is a scandal, all know, that there should be such a high proportion of people who remain illiterate, and an even higher number of people who read in such a rudimentary way that their intellectual development remains impeded. The result of this concern, the need to raise 'standards', naturally is to try to find solutions, to try to discover what is wrong and what to do about it. This is understandable, but the policy hysteria in which it is expressed can have damaging con-sequences.

One major impediment to reading, therefore, is the way it has become politicized. One sign of this is the number of different intervention programmes that are introduced. These can be categorized into three types. The first is the wider adoption of an approach that has already been piloted in a single local authority, or in a different country like New Zealand, which offers an element of training, and is seen to be the solution to all problems. The second is a huge investment in a new commercial reading scheme, offering a different approach that, while not guaranteeing success, at least guards against not attempting to overcome failure. The third type of intervention programme consists of those based on involving more sets of helpers, often parents, making sure that it is not just the beleaguered teacher who is the sole means of development.

There is little at fault with these approaches. They mean well. They usually work. And yet the magic does not seem to be there. The problem remains. Each approach has its virtues, but it also demon-strates fundamental flaws in a system that does not attempt to go to the heart of the problem.

Those researching the rise and fall of intervention schemes can probably list hundreds, some of which have attracted large-scale support. There is nothing wrong with their being very expensive, or that this expense is in addition to all the mainstream investment in teaching children. What is wrong is that each one is subject to politics and to fashion. They come and go. No sooner has one initiative been developed and become ripe for testing, than another has been introduced, distracting attention from the first. The political pressure is the need to claim personal success: 'This is my programme. I stake my future on it. I want all the glory myself', rather like Humpty Dumpty. Anything carried out with conviction can be successful. This is called the 'Hawthorn' effect: a new idea can be taken up with enthusiasm by people and, because it is new and believed in, be successful. Fashion is also a powerful element: the latest, the newest, the most up to date pervades the teaching of reading as much as anything else.

To repeat, there is nothing wrong with new intervention programmes. They are familiar and often sound. They can inspire the application of extra resources, and they can rekindle the enthusiasm of those who are doing their best at what sometimes feels like a thankless task. There are many clues about what could be useful in helping slow readers, and occasional insights into what their difficulties might be. But we should note that they are directed at 'slow' readers. These are remedial. These are designed for those who have failed. They might be used with all pupils, but children are not deceived. They are introduced because of failure. They are the response to problems, rather than a policy enabling success. The very fact that they are a change, an addition, draws attention to their status and their ephemeral nature. One is left reflecting sadly that there could be so much learnt and disseminated from them. But the political and fashionable signal remains, the assumption that there is only one solution and it is this.

The second example of intervention programmes is reading schemes. Here the term is used loosely, covering a range of materials that is either in book form or comprises other buyable equipment, like charts and letters and stands and wall displays. Again, the same grand rules apply. Different schemes are published, sold to schools and bought in the beliefs that not only such outside aids will help and support the teachers, but that they have a comprehensive theoretical base. The 'Hawthorn' effect can mean that the teachers, through their belief in the approach, are given renewed enthusiasm. The very fact that there is an investment in support gives a psychological boost. If there is a serious question hanging over the usefulness of these schemes, it is not because their theoretical approach is necessarily invalid. It is rather that their use can become routine and exclusive, and they may exclude other approaches that might be equally valid and more appropriate to some pupils, and that used to excess, many of them prove limited and boring.

Many reading schemes suggest that by using particular techniques, for example moving from mnemonics and associations to personal word-building, children will quickly grasp the secrets of reading. Rarely do they enable the analysis of the particular and personal art of reading to take place. The signal given is that adherence to a particular set of instructions will lead to automatic success. No disclaimers can overcome this effect on those who are using such schemes. The very fact that there is a given set of ideas or skills or instructions prevents teachers from using autonomy and relying on their insight to guide learners' development. The schemes should never rule out the use of alternative techniques, but they cannot be relied upon to be complete in themselves. Teachers often have good ideas about complementary techniques which can be used in conjunction with the schemes, and even when they do not, children can overcome that anyway.

The problem with reading schemes lies not in their good intentions but in the implication they carry that there is only one means through which pupils will learn. There have been many occasions when teachers have wrongly been led to presume that they, and only they, have the right to teach reading. Parents have often felt undermined by this, as if the very help that they have been giving is somehow counter-productive (when it is, in fact, essential). The idea that there is one particular technique that is so important that nothing else should exist is both doctrinaire and absurd. Its absurdity lies in the anomaly of the assertion. If it is so important why then is it so fragile, so easily undermined by other influences? Why should people be so naïve as to assume that the individual pupil coming to school can be so uncontaminated by previous experience? One might as well ask a parent to bring in a child without the ability to use language, in case that had also been learnt on 'wrong' principles.

There is another example of the power of simplistic doctrine. Those who have taught a long time can no doubt recall many examples of preachers, with all the zeal of limitations, espousing their particular cause. Individual schemes rapidly become forgotten, so it is worth recalling how much was invested in the initial teaching alphabet (ita). The principles on which this was based are very sound, and remain true. There is a problem between the number of sounds and the number of letters in the alphabetic system; indeed it is, at one level, *the* problem. The solution that was put forward and acted upon was to change the whole system of orthography, at least for those learning to read. George Bernard Shaw had suggested that the whole of the traditional spelling system should be changed, but the ita approach was more modest. It was proposed as a way of easing the introduction of the mechanics of reading. Once the pupil understood the simplicity of sight to sound correlation, 'hee cwd lrn tw reed'. Afterwards, a sudden translation to traditional orthography (TO) would be, so it was said, without trouble. The absence of books to read was deemed to be beside the point. Indeed, the very existence of stories and magazines and newspapers and signs in streets was ignored.

It seems many years since such schemes found such favour that they dominated some schools. It is worth repeating the last phrase: 'some' schools. The initiatives have been patchy and ephemeral. They have meant well, and have often provided more benefits than damage. Their danger is not so much that they divert energy and resources from real teaching but that they distract from more fundamental understanding.

Externally imposed initiatives have had the disadvantage of being both 'exclusive' and patchy: they are believed in strongly for a time and then forgotten. This is not unlike the experience of the third cohort of initiatives in the teaching of reading. These have to do with the support of, and for, parents and others in the development of reading. Nothing could be more significant than the involvement of parents, and nothing so useful as the engagement of an individual's attention. Why then does this often-repeated truth find its place in the section on 'impediments'?

Over the years there have been many schemes to involve adults and other children in the teaching of reading. When they have been evaluated they have almost invariably been shown to have positive results. In each case, some of the difficulties of persuading parents to find time, or overcome their reluctance, or of finding the means to bring about agreement between teachers and ancillary helpers, have been described in great detail. In each case we also had the sense that this was a new discovery. Those few, if any, who have read more than 150 reports, let alone the many that remain unrecorded, keep repeating this experience of discovery. For those taking part it is always new; it is always the first time. There is little sense of building on previous experience. Part of the policy hysteria, which relies on imposition on the one hand and a bidding system on the other, lies in this jumble of overlapping initiatives and new experiments, imposed even before the previous ones have come to a conclusion. It is as if the possibility of learning from experience – which is at the heart of reading – had been deliberately eschewed.

The involvement of parents is crucial. The more individual help a child can get, the better. The existence of books, the experience of stories, the possibility of dialogue, of conversation, of analysis, are all of such substance that their absence is the greatest impediment of all. About that a lot more could be done, but this enters the realm of politics, and even deeper issues about the early years of learning before formal schooling, and the role of parents as educators.

The politics of learning to read are a significant barrier to children. The problem is that politicians not only want rapid results, but wish to be associated with them. Someone else's ideas are inimical to this goal. The result is that the natural tension that lies at the heart of learning to read, between personality and experience, between individual psychology and methods of instruction, has become the stuff of fashion, with one side or another taken to pathological extremes. This is true of research as well as policy.

Research on reading has tended to reflect current fashions about reading. Some of the research is concerned with the underlying psychological processes; the other interest is with the pragmatics of reading, the testing of schemes or the evaluation of the role of parents. It is to be regretted that the two are rarely put together. At one time the diagnosing and treating of auditory and visual processes was seen as the great hope. Then there was a return to less academic factors, with a concern for reading instruction rather than perceptual training. Later the particular emphasis appeared to be on the role of the teacher. But rarely do we find a concern for understanding reading in the context of the inner world of the child. Reading is not an isolated skill. Its very complexity means that it should be seen in terms of children's grasp of the world. To that extent the realization that interaction with adults and a rich environment are important factors in reading is a welcome development.

The debate about the teaching of reading has centred on a particular way of expressing the dichotomy between perceptual and contextual approaches: 'phonics' or 'look and say'. Considering that neither approach can really explain the process of reading, and that even the Bullock Report relished the fact that there is no one scheme that answers all the problems of reading, it is disappointing that the traditional quarrel has continued so long. There are reasons why this is the case. Teachers need all the help they can get, and welcome what looks like a coherent 'scheme'. Any imposed scheme is bound to depend on a simplified notion of reading, and almost always needs to choose a specific approach. To say to teachers that there is nothing that can be done (a modern fashion) is not enough. Nor have teachers or parents been encouraged to learn all they need to learn about children themselves, and the way in which they come to terms with their world.

The dichotomy between 'whole words' and 'phonemes' is also an ancient one. The oldest method of learning to read was that of following closely (and inwardly digesting) passages from the Bible. Against such a scheme, it seemed obvious that it was better to teach children the alphabet so that they could spell out the necessary letters, like 'J' and 'o'. Since then, at one level or another, the argument against either one form of teaching or the other has continued unabated. The alphabet method was limited in not using words which made any sense. The 'whole word' method gave children no clues about how to begin to make sense of the word flashed before them. The yearning for a simple methodology remains, whether it consists of 'key words' or changing the alphabet to correspond to sounds, as in 'ita'. Teaching approaches and research reflect each other; the concerns with the technical aspects of reading, and particular stages of the decoding, were replaced by a stress on the idiosyncrasies of children and their motivation. The fact that reading (a 'psycholinguistic guessing game') is a combination of skills should help teachers to explore, more generally and sensitively, the particular nature of children's learning. Too often this concern for children's learning has marginalized the teachers.

Research on reading has merely fed the extremes of fashion that have led to so much pontificating about methodology. The emphasis on the idea that there is little to be done to enable children to read is inevitably replaced by the opposite extreme, that it is all a matter of one correct methodology. Some will have lived through a bombardment of methods, like colour coding, diacritical marking, flash cards and computer games. Many teachers have been undermined by fearing that their attempts to help were doing more harm than good. Rarely have teachers and parents been supported by insight and encouragement. The fear, 'Am I doing the right thing?', is often the means of preventing all the legitimate help and encouragement it is natural to give.

The greatest impediment, then, to the learning of reading is the disablement of those who are in the best position to help. Some parents do not have the resources to engage in sharing the act of reading, but even when they do have the time and resources, many feel shy about what they see as interfering in a technical subject. It is an interesting insight into the education system that this should be so. Such a lack of self-belief often affects teachers. It is a telling psychological fact that even after almost countless hours of being taught how to teach reading, there is a widely shared denial that anything ever took place. Teachers plead ignorance of the same technical experience. Why? What is it that undermines their self-belief, and their professional confidence? These are questions best left open. We are here concerned with what *can* be done.

We must recognize, nevertheless, that standards of reading at a variety of levels are lower than they should be. This need not be so. There are social and cultural barriers to the development of reading skills. Even well-intentioned policy initiatives can have the opposite effect. Knowing the impediments should again underline the essential principles.

- every attempt to help and encourage is worthwhile;
- it is not the child's personal fault if he or she has difficulties;
- it is never too early to teach 'reading' in the broadest interpretation of the term;
- it is never helpful to blame, except those who live by blaming.

Part two

Early reading

'She ought to know her way to the ticket office, even if she doesn't know her alphabet!'

(Lewis Carroll, *Through the Looking Glass*, Chapter 3)

Chapter 5
Auditory perception

Introduction

Children learn to read from the moment they are born. This assertion does not apply to the technicalities of decoding script and articulating recognizable phonemes, but to the necessary preconditions of reading. The abilities to make visual discriminations, to categorize and count, and to detect meaning in what is seen, are necessary prerequisites. So are the abilities to understand sounds, and to realize that some are more important than others, some more pleasant and some more meaningful. When parents talk to their babies, share sounds, and demonstrate the visual richness of the world, they are already teaching reading.

Whatever parents do with their children in terms of play and talk is good. There is no possibility of doing harm by introducing a 'wrong' method like the letters of the alphabet. Children will learn in their own ways, and will learn by discriminating between different techniques. As with computers, the more engagements that children have with them, the better. Their minds will not suddenly be trammelled by a particular experience.

Here we are discussing the necessary conditions for reading, both before the decoding of script and during the experience. The term 'pre-reading skills' used to be in fashion, but this is a misnomer. The skills of reading are auditory and visual, and the richer and more precise the experiences, like rhymes, the easier they are to apply to the peculiarities of script. Without language there is no reading, so there should be no sudden barriers that interfere with the experience. The skills of listening, talking and decoding need to be refined continually even when the reader has become fluent. This is the second reason why 'pre-reading' skills is not the right term. Many pupils who find reading difficult have not yet had the necessary grounding in visual and auditory experience, in listening to a variety of different voices pronouncing the same phoneme, or in detecting visual clues. These discriminations need to continue, and they deserve constantly to be refined, in art and music, as well as in poetry and drama.

Another term that used to be fashionable was 'reading readiness'. Again this is a well-meaning concept, implying that there are certain matters, like language, that are necessary conditions before reading can be learnt. The term also suggests a developmental stage that can clearly be differentiated. However, children are always ready to read. There is no point in forcing them or in suggesting that it is only at a particular moment, such as when entering school, that they should begin. They are constantly learning, interacting with their surround-ings, and engaged in seeking out dialogue and meaning. 'Readiness' is there from the start, a desire, not just a willingness, to learn.

A 'phoneme' is the unit of sound in any language that carries a distinct meaning to those listening. Until we know what sounds 'mean' we cannot even begin to make sense of what we hear, as those who have listened, say, to Far Eastern or African languages will know.

Auditory perception

To hear is easy. To listen carefully is less easy. To make sense of what we hear is more difficult still. To listen properly is to learn to develop the skills required for two tasks: to discriminate between those sounds that carry meaning and those that do not, and to translate those sounds into meaning. Many of the skills of listening are taken for granted once they are learnt; we ignore background music, or the sounds of traffic or airconditioning when we are concentrating on a conversation. We 'tune in' to listen to a particular voice when several people are talking at once. We can even 'reconstruct' what we have just heard when we realize that someone to whom we have not been listening has asked us a question. What we hear, therefore, is what we choose to hear; we have learnt to discriminate, so that we can take in one auditory message at a time.

Children's task of matching their understanding to the perceptual information being given is a complex one, for sound itself, and the way it travels, is not a simple matter. Noise has no fixed pattern; but is a complex wave-form in which the sound of speech is just one specific *type* of noise, called 'white noise'. But if sound is itself complex, the difficulty of deciding what to do with the sound is even more so. Every voice is recognizably different and yet uses uniform conventions to convey meaning. Children have to learn which particular sounds or suggestions of sound carry significance. Any study of phonemes, those sounds which signify distinct usable features in a language, shows how much needs to be learnt, although we are afterwards rarely aware of what we have been through to learn it. Some phonemes like 'p' and 'b' or 'k' and 'g' have only one small feature different from each other. Some distinctions of sound are particularly hard to learn, like 'th' in thick and 'th' in that. The varied use of the mouth to make sounds can cause difficulties in itself, some of which are never overcome as in the case of lisping, and in the difficulty of learning to pronounce another language.

The complexity of listening connects closely to subsequent abilities to learn to talk as well as read. There is a close connection between hearing, speaking and using a vocabulary. Children who are hard of hearing are symbolic of all children. For them, insight into the way in which language is organized and the way it is used to convey meaning through symbolic sounds is crucial. A number of decisions have to be made by each listener to judge each phoneme: the variables of speech, nasal or non-nasal, voiceless or voiced, sibilant or non-sibilant, are all elements that distinguish one phoneme from another. Distortions to the signal can get in the way of their proper reception, especially when the possible sound and meaning combinations are actually far greater than those used in any one language.

Some differences in pronunciation are quite subtle, but some are extreme, like the 'glottal stop'. This is the habit in some dialects of replacing the sound of the 't', as in 'glottal', with what is essentially a gap. In the cockney dialect, for example, the word 'glottal' tends to be pronounced without the central consonants, as 'glo'al'.

Young children slowly learn to distinguish some sounds from others, from the moment they pick out a familiar voice to the time when they have grasped the idea that sounds carry meaning. Even then, their progress towards discriminating between sounds is a fairly slow one: a typical one-year-old does not easily distinguish between 's' and 't', and later on children find difficulty with 'n' and 'm'. Children are innately responsive to sound frequencies in the same range as adult speech, but they then need to learn the significance of particular segments of sound used in their environment. As they get older they learn to associate sounds with particular events; they learn both to be pleased with sounds and to be frightened by them. They also learn how to pick out the significant message from a babble of noise, and to understand the message by the context in which they hear it.

Children's capacities to prefer familiar sounds to others, and to respond to differences in frequency, loudness and length of sound, are there from birth. They can localize sound and tell the difference between voices and other sounds. Children show an early preference for their mother's voice, and a clear dislike of any mismatch between a voice and a face. They also prefer some languages to others, even before they associate them with meaning. It is from this sense of the difference of sound that children learn to look for clues that can be identified as phonemes. Gradually the range of phonology builds up, until children have acquired the whole range of speech sounds. Children understand the significance of speech very early, and learn selective listening, knowing that the perception of continuous speech is different from the perception of isolated sounds. (People can detect sounds in words 100 times faster than any other sounds, such as the general noises of a town.) Although the development of distinctions between phonemes is not an easy process, very young infants can discriminate between syllables that differ only in one feature, as in 'pa' and 'a'.

Children are therefore quick to respond to the essential features of language, and have to learn to replace their own idiosyncratic interpretation with the consistent rules of phonology as they hear and detect them. Children reveal a systematic approach to understanding speech sounds, and at the same time reveal, by their difficulties, that the sounds they learn in their environment are neither universal nor innate. Their difficulty is in discovering the particular code being used, rather than in understanding the sense of language. Children use different strategies, quite systematically, for different conditions, trying to find a consistency of interpretation. They gradually learn to pick on the consistent features that matter in the packages of sound they hear. A phoneme is not just a sound, but a label for a class of sounds.

Children learn not just to hear, but to concentrate on those sounds that convey meaning. Their inner worlds are crowded with sensations of all kinds; they need to learn what is significant, what can be ignored and what has to be interpreted. Just as children learn to read not just by looking at the printed page but at the marks and the gaps between the words, so they need to hear the distinct sounds of speech. They learn to recognize those segments of sound with meaning, and to pick out such discrete units of sound from what is actually an indistinct continuous sound without clear breaks. We therefore teach children how to order what they hear. Monkeys and people have the same sensory capacities, but only people process speech.

One of the first abilities it is possible to extend in children is the ability to recognize a wide range of sounds, and to associate them with their source. We can use bells, or wooden blocks or even the noise of glasses humming when they are rubbed. We can extend children's ability to concentrate by asking them to recognize sounds played very quietly. A tape recorder can be very useful in seeing how many sounds children know without visual clues, sounds like the tearing of paper. Children can also pick out a picture illustrating a particular sound, and they can learn the meaning of sounds with which they might not be familiar.

Music can be a most useful means of teaching this awareness of sounds. Any musical instrument can extend aural discrimination. Records and tape recorders can be used not only to play different kinds of music, but can be associated with a particular scene, or with a story. *Peter and the Wolf* is the most famous example of the association between music and story, but children listen happily to any music that seems to convey a story. Even the recognition of the different instruments of an orchestra refines the ability to discriminate between sounds and to pay close attention.

If music is a natural aid to the development of listening skills, the voice is obviously more important still. Each person's voice has unique properties; and there is such a variety of dialects and methods of articulation that it is almost a wonder that people understand each other at all. When children learn to listen to voices, they identify first a sense of acoustic wave-forms, then linguistic features. They need to be encouraged to listen more carefully to features of speech that underlie the differences of pronunciation. They can learn to recognize different voices played on a tape recorder, and to recognize different accents saying the same thing. Young children are better at understanding tones of voice than they are at recognizing figures of speech, and this ability should be extended rather than ignored. They can learn to tell something about the mood of the person recorded, as well as picking out the same words spoken in a variety of accents and in a variety of ways. Just as they will quickly point out, in a story read for the tenth time, any deviation from the original, so they can learn to pick out any words changed in recorded sentences.

Training in listening to different voices is particularly helpful in the understanding of phonemes. Training in the development of rhythm gives the sense of spoken patterns as well as a clearer sense of listening and responding. Children can be asked to listen to and repeat rhythms made by tapping or clapping. They can clap in time to different pieces of music, or play percussion instruments in time with the music. They can also learn to associate the rhythms they hear with simple visual coding, so they see the connection between sound and script. Morse code can be a means of teaching children the connection between sight and sound, although clearly it can show no more than the distinction between long and short. Rhyme is a type of use of sound that draws attention to important phonemic features in a simple way. For young children, an understanding of rhyme is a sign that they have achieved a sense of the patterning of sound, which is why it is so popular with them. Like phonemes themselves, rhyme is a kind of convention in which we accept some sounds as being close together, and others, not that distinct, as not being close enough (like 'poem' and 'gnome').

Children's ability to pick out words that sound different and that are new to them is already a sign of their distrimination. They can pick out subtleties in a list of four or five words, or even differences in particular parts of words. They can make up rhymes of their own, and complete jingles and nonsense rhymes. They can pick out similar words in songs. They can associate the sound of words with visual symbols, by playing a version of 'snap' in which they put words with the same sounds together, like 'car' and 'star'; 'cat' and 'hat'. Alternatively they can use the same technique of sound associations in games like 'happy families'.

Children have a significant liking for word games and jingles that involve a patterning of sound. Children's associating abilities are shown in their own 'babbling' word games. Their liking for these derives from the fact that their understanding of language is reflected in their ability to recognize rhymes. Children can later discriminate in a more complex way by learning alliteration, where the sounds convey a sense of the meaning, and by putting together sentences or words that begin with the same sound. By the time they find this possible, however, the association of sound with meaning is already deeply embedded. Children also like to complete simple rhymes, like 'I like ham, butter and . . .'.

While we are teaching rhymes we are also conveying a sense of syllables, the ways in which words are structured. We can also teach children to discriminate more finely by encouraging them to 'place' sounds in the sources from which they come, and to pick out a particular sound in a jumble of other ones, with the same ability as a naturalist enthusing about the faint echoes of a lark against a fore-ground of the rumbling of heavy traffic on a motorway.

The development of auditory perception is never passive. Children's ability to remember verse and remember repeated sentences is an important part of their response to rhyme and rhythm. They can be encouraged to repeat particular sentences exactly, especially those sentences that are repeated in a story. Familiar phrases can be one of the most popular features in children's stories, with the sense of structure and context that such a device contains. The learning of nursery rhymes, with their emphasis on speech rhythms and clear sounds, is helpful as well as popular. This emphasis on auditory skills, from music to verses such as 'I know an old woman who swallowed a fly', is all at the service of teaching language generally, and phonemes in particular. Children learn not only rhymes but the individual sounds from which they are made. Children can learn to pick out particular consonants, like 's' and digraphs such as 'ch' in several words. Some stories can be constructed as a means of concentrating on particular sounds with which children might have difficulties. The sense of word endings and beginnings can be enhanced by asking children to begin a new word with the ending of a previous one. They can pick out particular sounds that appear as different parts of words, like 'in' or 'tion'. They then learn the idea that words are written, as well as spoken, as discrete units that then blend together.

By concentrating on the sounds of words, and more particularly on the convention of phonemes, children are learning many of the rudi-ments of reading. Every auditory game can be a means of developing this ability. 'I spy' is one useful game of auditory discrimination. Children will readily play games like 'filling the ark' when they must think of as many words beginning with a particular sound as they can, and will do so more readily than learning lists of phonics, such as 'tap, tin, tie, cup'. Listening to recorded stories helps children to listen carefully and learn to understand new words by the context in which they appear. Their ability to pay close attention to sounds as well as to their meanings is not a matter of fastidiousness but an essential skill they learn, and a skill that continues to be extended.

The knowledge of language and script depends on an awareness of the ways in which words are constructed. Children find it difficult to particularize words into sounds, which is why their ability to pick out the 'wrong' sound in a list of words such as:

thick, thistle, throw, fire, thimble

or

which, match, cash, each, latch

is so important. Some adults, after all, continue to have difficulty in discriminating between 'trap' and 'track'.

The connection between listening and speaking is a very close one: profoundly deaf children stop making sounds when they perceive no response from the outside world. The ability of children to listen to particular sounds is not always matched, however, by their ability to use these same sounds. Just as phonemes are generalized conventions that convey a symbolic sound despite differences in pitch, stress, tone and dialect, so children accept near equivalents to the words they wish to convey. This is well illustrated by the many accounts of how children think they are saying the same thing they hear, despite their inability to do so. There are also occasions when children realize that they cannot replicate the sound they hear:

Father: 'Say "jump".'
Child: 'Dup.'
Father: 'Jump.'
Child: 'Dup.'
Father: 'No, "jump".'
Child: 'Only Daddy can say "dup".'

The ability of children to listen is most actively enhanced by encouraging them to talk and responding to their talk. Babies want to express what they feel and to communicate something. They even use two different registers or tones of voice for the two tasks, as parents instinctively know from their experience. Their ability to use language goes through phases when, exploring all the phonetic licence possible, they appear to babble, and then when they limit themselves to the phonemes of their particular language. In this process of gradual concentration on a parody of the sounds that make a distinct language consistent, the parents have a significant role to play. Parents talk to their babies in unusual ways, varying their pitch much more than usual, even using higher frequencies. The degree to which parents respond to children's talk is a central factor in their language development, in transforming a baby's delight in babbling into a means of communication. The kind of response that parents make to their children varies so much that doubts are sometimes cast on whether such talk is useful to the child. But the language parents use, even when it sounds as if the baby is being treated like a pet, is important because it means that some kind of conversation is taking place; that language is being used. What children need is to have a response to the sounds they make.

Children's love of making sounds is the basis of their ability to discriminate between different sounds. Babbling gives them pleasure, since they are carrying out a form of parody of what they hear. They can, comparatively early, mimic typical patterns of pitch. But early forms of babbling are also persistent means of learning to control language by trying out different sounds and testing particular consonants or combinations. Children build up their phonological systems by making more and more precise differentiations. The sound of a language is a system that each child needs to learn so that he or she can use it. Children practise moving from small details of sounds to labyrinthine sentences, from general information to distinctions between consonants.

There are many ways in which children can be helped to develop their use of language. Given the concern that they should express what they mean to say, there is no need to limit our own vocabulary, or talk about the obvious. Their language will develop according to their need to convey ideas and emotions. When children are heard as well as seen, fruitful use should be made of their talk. Speaking and listening should always go hand in hand. Children's articulacy is founded upon the discipline of listening. Even with adults, keeping 'the conversational ball rolling' is a skill, not always widely shared.

Children can learn how to use language clearly by relating simple instructions. Descriptions of unseen objects that are sufficiently clear for other people to understand the references are never easy to perform, because we all have the tendency to use general gestures rather than precise descriptions. Children can be asked to describe an object in such a way that other children can try to picture what they are told. Alternatively, children can be given pictures of four different faces and asked to describe one of them in such a way that it is clear to anyone having duplicate pictures which one is being particularized. Children can also be asked to describe what they imagine is conveyed in a picture, half of which is covered up, or what might happen next in a story they are being told. The ability to give directions how to find a house or street, or how to find where an object is hidden in a room, without simple pointing, is a complex task that all can find challenging.

Clarity of expression and confidence in the use of language derive not just from the ability to give instructions, but from encouraging children to communicate what they think or feel about things. The conditions for such help are often not easy to achieve, because of lack of time. Because of the numbers of children in primary school class-rooms, for example, and despite teachers' desire to listen to each child read individually, the amount of attention paid to each during the day averages around one minute. Yet children want to talk, and are often engaged in very important conversations with each other. One researcher who wished to record the natural conversation of children hit upon the idea of giving them a white rabbit to look after, telling them that it would go mad unless it heard the constant sound of human voices. The children had no difficulty in 'soothing' the rabbit for hours.

Children's use of language can be helped through their ability to carry out parodies of what they hear. Even very young children are adept at taking off adults playing certain roles. The use of puppets can help children play different roles and extend the needed uses of language, just as they can be encouraged to carry out certain forms of drama by playing the roles of mother or father or other adults. The natural delight children have in dolls and toy soldiers (itself a signif-icant insight into the way in which they learn to adjust to the world) is a useful starting-point for more extended dialogue. Children talk both when they have something interesting to say and when they talk for the sake of talking. Both deserve a responsive listener to help them develop their self-confidence. The subject matter, be it television programmes or a story, is not as important as the fact that children should not only passively receive information, but convey it.

Chapter 6
Visual perception

Children learn to read from the moment they are born. Their recognition of shape, and the translation of shape into meaning, for example by familiarity when they respond to their mother's face, is the first stage of their adaptation to a world of symbols and images. What children see depends on their interpretation of what they see. They learn to focus and they learn through their experience to make sense of what they see. After a time it is almost impossible to revert to that innocent gaze which does not automatically interpret what is seen according to previous experience. For us, it is impossible to look at even a simple sign without using some interpretation. In this picture the top horizontal line of these two looks larger because of our familiarity with perspective:

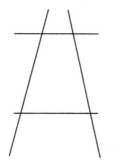

We have, after all, seen railway lines going into the distance, and even if we *know* that the two horizontal lines are the same length (because we tell you they are, and you can measure them) they do not look the same. Again, if we take another example, one of the vertical lines looks longer than the other:

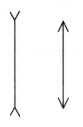

Again, you can measure them. But do they not seem different? Why? What experience do we have that impinges on our vision? In the following picture, which is the dent and which is the bulge?

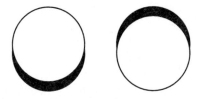

Do they look the same, being mere flat black-and-white shapes on the page, or do we interpret them differently? Does not our instinctive awareness of light and shadow mean we see them as distinct?

Every act of reading is a form of interpretation, a visual sense of significant clues, including the two-dimensional aspect of reading and the importance of the right 'point of view'. We remember that the letter 'd' can only be read when it is that way up. Children learn to recognize recurring signs whenever they appear, and learn how to make sense of the array of perceptions around them. The power of the brain over the eye is best illustrated by two familiar examples when we 'see' the same thing but interpret it in different ways. The 'Neckar cube' can be seen from two separate perspectives:

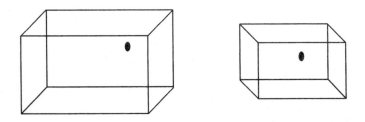

The dot can be seen to be either at the front of the box or at the back. The eye sees one thing; the brain chooses to interpret either one thing or the other. Similarly, the eye responds to the following simple picture, but the brain can interpret it as either a duck or a rabbit, especially if I say it could be either:

Look from left to right and then the other way round. The most significant fact about visual perception is that it needs to be learnt, and is a matter of constant interpretation.

From the first moment of their entry into the visual world, children are fascinated by what they see, and will stare constantly at whatever surrounds them. This interest is an early sign of learning, for they show far greater interest in faces than in any series of squiggles. Soon children respond not just to any face but to familiar ones, and are frightened by pictures where the familiar is distorted, responding happily to:

or even the same face upside-down, but disliking a picture in which an eye is missing:

Although young babies find it more difficult in perceiving perspective to interpret what they see, simply because their eyes are closer together, they nevertheless demonstrate the ability to understand depth perception and size constancy. One famous example of this inborn sense of visual significance is a particular experiment in which babies were tempted to crawl towards their mothers across a glass that covered a hole. Because the pattern that was used on the sides and the bottom of the hole looked so alarming, the babies would not cross it. They made sophisticated visual judgements rather than relying on touch.

In addition to their ability to learn how to follow the presumed path of a moving object and therefore anticipate events, babies reveal a systematic quality in their visual exploration, looking at corners and edges, focusing on parts of objects rather than vaguely scanning whatever is before them. If children suffer from perceptual deprivation in early childhood, their later learning is severely affected. The ability is there. They can count even before they use language in the fullest sense.

Visual perception depends as much on the brain as it does on the eyes themselves. We actually receive an image of the world upside down, and yet the world does not look upside down because our brain automatically translates the image into being the right way up. It is possible to fit mirrors on to glasses and turn the world upside down. After several days the brain is no longer so confused and adjusts. Just like G M Stratton in 1897 who first tried the experiment, all who wear these devices get used to the inverted image in about a week. It also takes them about a week to readjust to the 'normal' or 'real' perception of the world. The distinction between the actual and the perceived qualities of the environment is crucial. However we judge it, one of the following shapes looks larger than the other.

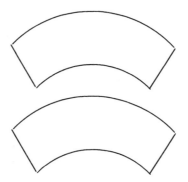

There is a tendency for perception to be biased in favour of simplicity and stability, and away from any complexity or instability. Children learn perceptual constancy, seeing the environment as constant, as in the case of someone walking away into the distance but being seen as remaining the same size, just as they learn colour constancy.

The perception of stimuli depends on the amount of stimulation already present: the stronger the original stimulus, the greater difference there needs to be before any change is perceived. A single candle in a dark room, for example, has quite a different effect from one more candle in a room in which one hundred other candles are already burning. Babies need to learn not only the essential constancies of perception, that objects remain the same from wherever they are viewed, but also the concept of objects, that they exist out of sight and touch, and that they each have a unique identity. Babies acquire the knowledge of the permanence of people before they are aware of the permanence of objects. Later perceptual development is just as complex and just as important, despite our tendency to take it for granted.

Visual perception is not a matter of passive reception, like template matching. Nothing could be more different from the way in which a computer can select information than the way people do so. We have more difficulty picking out a shape like this:

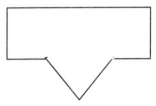

from (a) or from (b) than we do from (c):

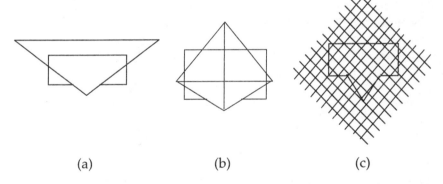

| (a) | (b) | (c) |

Machines find equal difficulty with (c), but our perception is also affected as much by other stimuli as by a sense of meaning in shapes. If people are presented with a shape – like this:

and interpret it, or hear it called a particular object, they will remember it according to the label it has been given, and reproduce it later, not as they saw it, but as they remember the label: pickaxe, or anchor, or mushroom. People reproduce not what they remember having seen, but what they remember having interpreted. The world of perception is one in which the idea of what is 'real' remains complex, since what people perceive is what they think is real. For young children this is not just a philosophical question. They are learning to interpret and to use their eyes in particular ways. Their eyes, like the eyes of all adults, are in constant motion. The eye keeps drifting off course even when ostensibly fixed on an object, moving about the target between two and five times per second. When people read they look at a text in a series of jumps mostly from left to right, which take place between three and four times per second. In this continual movement the perception of objects depends more on the attitude of the observer than the nature of what is observed. Exposure for as little as 50 milliseconds is enough for most information to be taken in and processed.

Children need to organize what they see. This organization is the ability to make sense of a series of perceptual clues that, once under-stood, is thereafter simple, but until that moment seems impenetrable. If we are confronted with a simple pair of pictures we might not at first see what they symbolize.

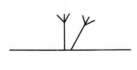

However, once we have been told that the first illustrates an early worm catching a bird and the second is of a giraffe passing a window, we are apt to recognize them immediately thereafter.

Handwriting presents particular difficulties. The difference between a word written:

and one written

is a small matter of joining parts together: the small matter that makes all the difference, although most of the same essential clues are present in both.

The connection between visual perception and reading is so close that there is even a definite association between measures of visual perception and specific tests of reading. This is not only because reading depends on visual clues, but because the brain is similarly engaged in both tasks. The choice between two interpretations of this picture:

which can be seen as a goblet or two profiles of people looking at each other, has its linguistic equivalent in sentences that can be organized by the brain in two ways:

What upset Bill was looking at Mary.

Either Bill was upset looking at Mary, or someone else who was upsetting him was doing the looking.

Children's ability to perceive develops rapidly, if not always constantly, until they can interpret newspaper and television images as well as the significance of particular shapes. Generally, at around the age of 18 months they understand two-dimensional representations; after that children learn to match small toys to pictures. When they are very young they have momentary interests; they then fix their interest on one object for longer, until they learn new focuses with faster changes of attention. They then learn integrated attention to two things at once. But one should not assume that there are certain stages through which they should go. Complex visual tasks can be interspersed with simple ones, partly because children need the juxtaposition of the familiar and the unfamiliar, and partly because it is not always easy to judge difficulty. Five distinctive visual features are enough to distinguish all the letters of the alphabet, but this simplification, if true, draws attention to the complexity of interpretation that arises from so few clues.

Young children constantly need to refine their visual perception. Their problem is not that they see too little, but too much. They need to learn to pick out significant details from a crowded visual world, to see the significance of the symbolism of two dimensions. The interpretation of pictures is itself an important part of visual education. Children can be asked to discuss simple pictures that can be explained, or complex pictures that demand refined attention, especially if the picture is studied closely rather than glanced at. Children can also look for particular objects in a picture, which may be deliberately hidden or camouflaged, and may be unfamiliar to them. Pictures with several hidden objects are always useful. It is also worthwhile asking children to 'extract' the distinct items from a picture in which real objects or abstract figures are juxtaposed:

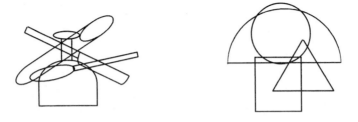

Children are often better at interpreting incomplete pictures than real ones, even when one might think that the 'minimalist' art of a cartoon should be harder to see than the richer completeness of a colour photograph. One way of teaching visual discrimination is by comparing two pictures that are slightly different in their details, a game often used as an adult amusement or competition. Children can also look at pictures with an awareness of their style – the way they are drawn, the way the light is used in a photograph – for all these differences are significant. Discussions about pictures do not need to be concerned only with what they represent. Children can be asked to interpret complex semi-abstract pictures or each other's drawings. They are often rather better at seeing what the creator intends to communicate than are adults.

Once children are able to define and interpret pictures, it is far easier for them to pick out the significance of particular shapes. They can practice their sense of standard letters by picking out the odd one in an otherwise standard sequence like this:

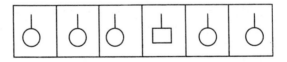

They can be asked to develop this ability through increasingly difficult examples, through letters:

to words:

From this ability to pick the odd one out, they can go on to group objects by shape, size or colour, developing that important ability to understand the concept of classifications. They can also learn to continue visual sequences such as:

$$\bigcirc - \bigcirc - \bigcirc - \quad /\,\backslash\,/\,\backslash\,/\,\backslash\,/\,\backslash$$

until some sequences could be quite complex:

$$\square \;\times\; \bigcirc \;\bigcirc\; \square \;\times\; \bigcirc \;\bigcirc\; \square$$

They could also arrange cards of different shape and colour into as many different variations as possible:

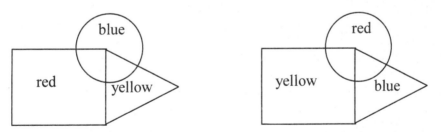

Children's ability to match shapes or letters can be helped by games of dominoes, or any sequences of cards that can be placed together to make pictures when joined. This can be in the form of a straight line of cards like this:

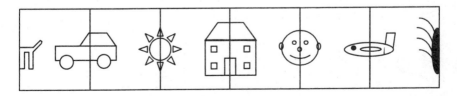

or in the form of a complete circle. The game of dominoes can be played using pictures or simple shapes as well as dots.

The ability to match shapes can be developed by requiring children to copy shapes. They can, for example, copy an outline like this with building blocks:

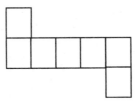

They can also be asked to carry out more sophisticated versions of this by reversing or inverting the design.

Whereas babies are disturbed by the slightly unfamiliar, slightly older children like to be presented with games of mismatch as well as matching. They can pick out what is obviously false in a picture, such as a horse with five legs, or a man with six fingers. They can build up a picture by putting different parts of it together, whether as a simple jigsaw, or as a combination of different parts of the body:

especially when there are many potentially absurd results. Children can also be asked to finish pictures in which there is obviously a part missing.

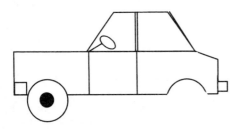

The ability of children to draw can be used as a test of their sense of symmetry, proportion, size and organization. The integration of different parts into a whole can be varied by the juxtaposition of bizarre combinations of parts like a beard or moustache, or different hats or footwear.

Almost any kind of picture can, when cut up and rearranged, make a useful jigsaw. Jigsaws can be kept as simple as matching two halves, or they can be made complicated. The matching of shapes can also be made increasingly demanding by asking children to fit parts to complete a picture, or a shape.

Children can also be asked to copy simple shapes with small sticks or matches:

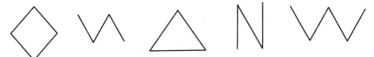

Children's ability to interpret what they see can be helped on a variety of levels. If a wire clothes hanger is twisted into a clear shape and shown to children at an angle, they can be asked to match what they see to the same shape seen from the front. Children can be asked to spot familiar objects photographed from unusual angles. They can say what several objects would look like when seen from different angles. They can also match a picture to an object by putting the object into the same position as is shown in the picture.

Children's visual perception extends from the interpretation of complex material, like an oil painting, to the understanding of simple shapes symbolizing actual objects.

Children need to learn the use of symbol in drawings, from simple cartoons in comics to those in newspapers. Newspaper photographs are not easy to read at first, consisting as they do of series of dots out of which shapes can be recognized. Pictures relying on patterns of shadow and light are particularly interesting for analysis. Slides shown out of focus can test how minimal are the clues needed for their interpretation. But correct focusing is itself a sophisticated visual art, and every time young children are encouraged to look at pictures, objects or games, they are learning both perspective and focusing.

The teaching of colour is important because recognizing colour is a matter of using symbols as well as perception. The concept of 'red' includes a wide range of different colours, from cherry blossom to sunsets. We have the variations of 'scarlet', 'pink' or 'crimson', but inhabitants of the Kalahari desert have 23 different words for 'red'.

Perception depends on memory, on memory learnt by recognition of the familiar. Children build up their knowledge of the world not by recalling every image at will, but by recognizing those they have seen before. The love of repeated stories, familiar faces and known toys is all part of a process of creating a familiar and understood world. Visual perception also implies the development of memory, and this itself can be helped. One of the most obvious and useful means is 'Kim's game', where children are shown familiar objects or shapes, which are then covered up, and the children are asked to remember all the objects that they saw. They can also be asked to spot which object has been taken away from a group. At a more difficult level they can play a game with cards in which the pack is laid out face downwards and cards are turned over two at a time by different players. Those who match a pair keep them; those who turn over unmatching cards are asked to turn them back face downwards. Those who remember the denomination of cards that have been displayed and replaced will match the most cards. Children can be asked to describe all the details in a picture that they see for a short time, assessing how fast they can observe all the minutiae, and how clearly they can describe them. This can be made into a game, concentrating on different colours, or seeing how short a glimpse is the minimum necessary for remembering. Children have a great capacity for observation, as is seen in their recall of details of television programmes when they are asked beforehand to pay attention, but this capacity is rarely used.

Children can be helped to observe closely by paying attention to a variety of stimuli, from solid objects to television programmes or computer games. It is only when they share what they see with others, when they are asked to describe what they have seen, that such 'critical' observation is developed. Otherwise, the more they see, the less they take in. Close visual attention and description is also much more fun than the indifferent response to a parade of images. Simple card games like 'snap' demand accuracy as well as speed, and can also be adapted to include letter shapes. One alternative to 'snap' is the game in which whoever first spots an agreed card like the Jack when it is turned face up wins all the cards previously revealed.

The recognition of similar elements, which can be approached through a variety of techniques, is a fundamental aspect of many stages of learning, since it includes the bases of categorization and recall. The clues to be recognized can be made increasingly subtle and complex, and can require the skill of reproducing figures or shapes. The ability to decode pictures can be extended at a variety of levels, including conjecturing which colours are suggested in black and white pictures, and unusual subjects. A series of pictures can be put into a logical sequence, creating a sensible storyline. Children can also work out ways of reversing figures; instead of reproducing exactly a shape with building bricks they can be asked to set it out in different directions, converting the vertical to the horizontal and vice versa.

Chapter 7
Psychomotor skills

The term 'psychomotor skills' sounds both grand and mechanical. It is simply a way of drawing attention to those matters we tend to take for granted, like the relationship between the mind and the body. If the brain can reinterpret what we see, what is so palpably there, then it can affect the very physical habits of the everyday, and vice versa. There are so many things we take for granted in reading, like the way our eyes move, or the assumed correlations between visual symbols and meaning. We are complex creatures. We are not just cognitive learning machines. We are, to use the old-fashioned term, 'instinct' with instincts. The term 'psychomotor' is grand, drawing attention to this complexity. It is also mechanical in so far as we do so many things without thinking. It is not just habit, but something taken for granted.

The relationship between mind and body is very close, and even in childhood the connection is obvious. Children first learn to understand the world not only by making sense of what they see and hear, but by their ability to use their physical skills, like focusing and grasping. The development of the body is linked to every other development of understanding. This is why some commentators have been tempted to explain human beings in terms of distinct stages, as if all could be seen as clearly as physical growth. The relationship between the inner and outer worlds of children, as of adults, remains a complex one. The ability to stretch out and hold on to an object is both an assertion of individuality and a sense of the objective nature of the world. It is difficult to develop one without the other.

Reading obviously depends upon physical abilities; but some of these are less obvious than others. Just as a hearing or sight impairment may not be obvious until careful diagnosis, so the inability to balance, to develop sophisticated coordination, or a sense of left and right, might be a hidden impediment to the learning of reading. Physical development is a matter not just of possessing the necessary abilities, without which reading would be impossible, but of developing them continually. This is why the 'sixth' sense, called 'proprioception', the sense that tells us where the mobile parts of our bodies are in relation to the rest, is so important. That automatic memory, the ability to coordinate, has to change constantly as the child grows bigger.

Babies a few days old not only take in sounds and sights but can imitate the movements of a face, and are able to locate sounds. They also understand that there is a source for a sound, something to look for. The ability to fix the eyes on a particular target is a physical skill that is not used all the time, since adults' eyes keep drifting off course and only move on to a precise target, like a word, fleetingly. All people are better at seeing things at long range rather than in close-up. Reading places many demands on children's psychomotor skills. Even focusing alternately between distant and near objects needs to be learnt.

Early reading

The basic concept of 'reading readiness' came about because of the obvious need for physical coordination and the understanding of language, before any kind of reading can be begun. But it also derives from the suggestion that it is necessary to wait for natural development to take place before any teaching is done, and from the idea of distinct stages in development. The fact that many children learn despite being taught that maturity itself is important, makes the concept of 'readiness' attractive, but nowadays it is a term that is generally found unhelpful. This is because it is clear that children can learn to read in the formal sense far earlier than the age of six and a half suggested by Pestalozzi, who first used the term in 1925. It is also clear that children are learning to read in the wider sense from the moment they are born. The concept of reading readiness, really early reading, draws attention not just to growth or maturation but to the achievement of prior learning on which new learning can be based. It is for this reason that so much stress is being placed on the early skills. The move from the use of language, and the coordination of psychomotor abilities, to the understanding of reading, is so complex that it is impossible to separate one from the other.

Coordination

Children who suffer from reading disabilities have difficulty in connecting sounds and visual clues, such as matching rhythmic taps against the reproduction of patterns. Both require the translation of a sequence in space into a sequence in time, and both depend on the coordination of different senses. This ability to put together different concepts can be fostered by the development of tactile senses. For this reason there are many tests designed to diagnose the essential ability to understand symmetry, size and proportion, not only recognizing them but being able to manipulate them. The 'drawing a man' test is designed to explore children's ability to integrate and organize. The 'visual-motor Gestalt test', in which a child is asked to copy 9 figures, explores the ability to reproduce, and the understanding of reversals. The 'visual retention test' gives children 10 seconds to look at a design before they reproduce it. The 'block design' tests children's ability to complete an unfinished design. All of them are concerned with the ability to coordinate more than one skill.

Categorization

Underlying the ability to make sense of coordination is the fundamental cognitive skill of categorization, the understanding of classes of objects, by which process the world can be understood in a manageable way. There are many ways, both cognitive and semantic, in which children can be helped to develop their reading abilities through categorization, but all of them involve physical manipulation in one way or another. Even playing with dolls, like the matching of pictures and objects, is a way of developing symbolic understanding. All kinds of matching abilities, whether of colour, shape or words, are important, since classification is essential for any type of thought. When children are playing with their toys, therefore, they are extending not only their physical skills but their intellectual skills as well.

Developing physical abilities

The most obvious forms of physical coordination need to be encouraged and extended. Balancing is itself an important physical ability which, as we know from tightrope walking, can be trained beyond normal needs. To walk along a narrow plank is not as easy as it looks.

We can enable children to learn this task by arranging planks at right angles. We can ask children to balance books on their heads. We can see if they are able to stand astride the pivot of a small see-saw by distributing their weight in the right way. We can ask children to do other more complex tasks than balancing. We can give complicated instructions to follow, to test the ability not only to carry out a physical task, but to do so in the right sequence. We can use drama as a way of developing coordination: simple scenes with clear and precise physical action, demonstrating the point of a story. This can be developed in terms of a mime, the expression of an emotion or idea. Any form of dance extends the physical control of children. Some forms do more; they give the physical abilities some point. We can ask children to explore problems by experimenting. One simple example is seeing how it is possible to reach an object that is higher than anyone can stretch.

Skills of manipulation

All the ideas suggested so far are for the development of general coordination, but there are many activities that relate more obviously to reading. The ability to have control, not only over the senses, but over the arms and the fingers, is obviously necessary. Clumsy movements indicate a lack of physical focus. We need to develop physical abilities as much as possible, so that children can look closely and work delicately. Any activity that encourages refinement of movement will help. The unravelling of a maze of string is another test of the child's ability to unravel a maze of lines on paper: although one is a three-dimensional task and demands physical skills, and the other is two-dimensional and more a matter of concentrated eye movements, both make intellectual demands. Any kind of tracing demands coordination. The tracing of a picture teaches control over finger movement. The tracing of an outline or map is, after all, not easy for older children. If we can teach this, we are teaching the ability to concentrate, as well as the ability to form letters. Children can be asked to draw a pencil line between two other lines:

They can also be asked to see if they can move a ring around a piece of wire without them coming into contact. Versions of this game can be purchased, usually devised so that when the ring and wire touch an electrical circuit is completed and a bell rings, but it is possible to construct a more simple version by hand. The tracing of letters in sand, and familiarization with a particular shape through touch, suggest similar control. The sand box can be put to constructive use. Children can be asked to trace a particular shape in the sand, for example copying a figure that the teacher traces on the child's back.

The use of toys

Toys are by their very nature 'educational', a part of experience that children use in their development. Any number of objects can be used in helping to develop psychomotor skills. The matching of shapes and colours is an important task, especially when there are variations in size between objects that are the same shape, making children look for the significant differences. Children can be asked to identify the materials of different objects, to classify them by texture or weight as well as by shape and size. Models of cars can be categorized according to a number of different criteria, from colour to type. The development of tactile abilities can be encouraged by asking children to identify different objects by touch. A box (like a lucky dip) containing different objects can be used until children not only identify each object hidden inside it, but also recognize the familiar ones quickly. It is because of the importance of this type of physical control that various types of building block are so useful.

Any kind of building game, constructing, balancing, making definite shapes, even to the point of repetition, provides the kind of exercise that children instinctively realize is useful, and go on pursuing themselves. This instinctive feeling is significant, and can be encouraged by asking the child to work out exactly a sequence of tasks that become ever more complex. One of the variations on building with blocks is for children to make models, either out of Plasticine (a difficult medium) or out of interconnecting plastic or metal pieces (such as Lego or Meccano). Children can also be asked to create a model that suggests the scene of a story. It does not need to be elaborate, but can be something that merely suggests enough for others to guess what it signifies. It is, of course, also possible for a class to make a more elaborate model as a collective effort, perhaps to illustrate the general scene of a series of stories, or to make a complete 'world'. But generally it is important to encourage a more immediate use of manipulative skills. Lego and other similar construction games are useful aids. Even cutting out pictures from a paper, or from comics to make up a story, requires a distinct skill. Any drawing, painting or colouring is a way of communicating and a way of learning to master the techniques involved in reading and writing. Tracing in sand or in other materials can suggest more directly the shapes and meaning of letters.

Children's ability to categorize can also be extended by asking them to describe foreground and background, and their ability to coordinate developed by asking them to 'track' a line on a wall with a torch. Drawing is an important way of teaching children how to hold a pencil, how to control lines, how to form shapes and how to translate an idea into two dimensions. The ability to join a series of dots, which later can be in the shapes of letters, is one form of 'controlled' drawing. Children can also be asked to reproduce simple outline drawings from memory. They can be asked to trace patterns, made up either of simple repeated shapes or of more complex figures:

Tracing is as helpful to the development of psychomotor skills as jigsaws are to visual coordination and interpretation. Many games, such as cat's cradle, have long been used as a way of helping children develop intricate manual skills. The game of spillikins, where children take out one stick at a time from a jumbled heap without disturbing the rest, or building blocks into as high a tower as possible, also help to develop delicate physical control. The old game of 'Jenga', taking as many pieces as possible from a tower of wooden blocks, without the whole edifice collapsing, is another example.

Left to right orientation

English is written from left to right. This is a simple mechanical fact that needs to be learnt by everyone in the initial stages of reading. It is not a habit that comes automatically, even if it is difficult for adults familiar with the concept to comprehend that such a basic fact needs to be taught. But the fact that we write from left to right is arbitrary. To a society dominated by the idea of the right-handed, and a suspicion of the left (sinister) side, it might seem that our language evolved out of physical ease, but we could just as well be writing from right to left, as in Hebrew or Arabic, or from bottom to top as in Chinese or Japanese. We happen to have chosen a particular convention, which children need to learn, together with the fact that we start our journeys through left to right at the top of the page and work down to the bottom.

The left to right orientation symbolizes a number of important facts about reading. The ability to convey meaning depends on physical conventions. We cannot really separate the skill from its significance, the mechanical from the semantic. And the left to right orientation demonstrates the importance of being able to organize information into a coherent pattern by ignoring certain parts of it. We limit ourselves to a particular dimension until we think of it as automatic. For a child, however, this ability to organize by concentration on one thing rather than another is a basic conceptual leap, especially as its conventions and discriminations are nearly always based on limitations. We use two dimensions in reading, and not three. The left to right orientation is a matter not just of whole words but of individual letters. An animal remains an animal whether seen from below, above or behind; but the letter 'p' is only significant when seen from one direction. Most letters are distinguishable from each other by a shift of direction; 'b' and 'd' for example. This difference is not easily spotted by children, unless they have a thorough grounding in awareness of two significant dimensions.

As teachers, our main concern is to help children use the concept of left and right, as car drivers use the concept both automatically and when following an instruction. The concept underlying reading, and the distinction between top and bottom, must become automatic so that children do not need to think consciously about it. We need to give them as much practice as possible in using techniques that foster awareness of the concepts, even before they read. Any reading from a book can be accompanied by following the text with the finger. We can ask the child to give us the book to read the correct way up. We can encourage the basic handling of a book by showing children books with pictures in a story sequence; or cartoons that can be followed through. We must always try to make children aware of the beginnings both of words and of sentences. We can encourage the sense of left and right by asking them to copy drawings in that direction, always moving their eyes from the picture on the left to the reproduction on the right.

Much practice in internalizing the left to right sequence can come from simple games. Using a pegboard we can ask children to complete various kinds of sequence from left to right, either with different colours or with different shapes. We can ask them to reproduce patterns out of verticals and horizontals. Using drawing pads, children can emulate simple patterns like a series of dots and dashes from left to right. They can reproduce simple letter shapes, again in sequence. We can ask them to thread a sequence of alternate cubes or beads. When we wish to demand something more complex we can use the pegboard or paper to ask children to make sequences of lines in different areas, to emphasize the difference between top and bottom as well as left and right. Once children are quite clear about the difference between vertical and horizontal, we can also teach them how to reproduce diagonal lines, and indeed some of the other basic shapes out of which letters are formed, such as curves and circles.

We do not need to emphasize the left to right sequence merely in terms of simple shapes. We can show children a series of cards with pictures on them, say of a house, a car and a plane, and ask them to put them into the sequence of a story that mentions them, or into a sequence that was previously shown to them. Children can also put a series of cards into a logical sequence, as with three cards consisting of a man walking, getting on a train and sitting in the carriage with the train moving. The concept of order and its link with left to right sequencing can also be enhanced by asking children to remember a series of words and reproduce them in the same order. When the teacher then dictates any sequence, say of dots and dashes, children should be able to write it down fluently and without difficulty.

Every discussion of a child's picture of the illustrations in a book can be accompanied by frequent questions about what is on the left or right-hand side. Children can be asked to pick out pictures that are upside down, or shapes that differ because they are back to front. The connection between this basic orientation and letter shapes is, after all, very close. Children can also be asked to make a long line with bricks, using as many different shapes (vertical, diagonal, etc) as they can. It is also useful to teach children the difference between clockwise and anticlockwise. In all these exercises children are learning a basic skill on which writing depends. It is an arbitrary convention that they are learning, but they need to internalize it as if it were natural.

Chapter 8
Attitudes to reading

Some children learn to read with such ease that it is difficult to understand how they acquired the art. Some children learn to read despite being encumbered with inappropriate help. One important factor that contributes to early learning, and helps children to avoid later, more difficult struggles with the skills needed for reading, is recognition of the purpose of reading. This tends to underpin the entire enterprise, and in turn underlines the importance of creating an environment in which reading is the most natural and enjoyable activity. Each child's ability to learn is best helped by giving that child a purpose. Print is not such a barrier if it is seen as a means to an end, rather than a mystery in itself. When children see beyond a task to the reason for carrying it out, then learning the intermediate task is that much easier.

Reading as pleasure

Stories are an extremely important means of conveying ideas about the world. For this reason alone children should want to learn to read, so they can have the pleasure of stories whenever they wish. It is through the recognition of this that certain traditional reading schemes are attacked. Instead of a story that makes sense, children are confronted with sentences that, even if phonically simple, do not provide the kind of material that many people would *choose* to read:

> I can fan a sad man. I can fan a tan man. I can fan a bad man. Can I fan a mad man?

Reading is not just a matter of the instrumental, of being able to recognize signs like 'Police' and 'Stop'. Nor is a matter of recognizing flash cards with sentences like these on them:

Mother I am wet.
Dora has Jane.
I am Fluff the cat.
Dick has the dog.
It will get well.

For children, reading only makes sense when there is a clear purpose for it and when they see that purpose. Only then will the intermediate difficulties be overcome.

It is, of course, the intermediate skills, between the understanding of language and the development of reading, that cause problems. There are many attempts to combine the phonetically simple with interesting material, as in the use of nonsense verse and nursery rhymes. But whatever approach is used, children need to understand the pleasure to be derived from books. For many children the great problem has been that reading is not associated with pleasure. Primary school children consistently discriminate between valuing reading and enjoying it. They are *told* it is important, so they see it as a task they must undertake. In the Assessment of Performance Unit's survey of reading, it was discovered that 80 per cent of children preferred reading at home rather than at school, and that half of them had difficulty in finding suitable books to read in school. Two-thirds disliked having to express opinions about what they had read. It is hard for children to learn anything when learning is associated with painful labour, and all pleasures are associated with lack of thought. Young children at home think of reading as book-aided story repetition; at school they then are confronted, almost as a separate part of the curriculum, with the encoding of print.

The purpose of reading

Children's developing sense of their environment can be easily seen when they are first learning how to gesture, and to copy what they hear. Many of their guesses at meaning are more complex inter-pretations than parents realize, from the idea of perspective to the understanding of symbols. In the interplay between expectation and observation and the constant experiments they need to make, the idea of the translation of a spoken language into a visually recorded form is one of the most difficult. Very young children have great difficulty in seeing the purpose of writing, and need to learn that books contain stories. Many of the technical matters of reading, including the concepts of 'word', 'letter' and even 'writing', are only vaguely understood. Without an awareness of what reading entails it is hard for children to understand the central task of reading. This is especially anomalous since children are at the same time carrying out far more complex tasks in language, such as understanding a word as abstract: as 'thought'. The purpose of reading and the essential skill involved should not be too difficult to convey. The association of a story with a particular book, and the knowledge exactly which words appear on which page (children will quickly point out if you get it wrong), itself demonstrates to children what books are for.

Parents and reading

The most important gift that parents can give their children is the association of reading with pleasure. The role of parents in all the early reading skills is obviously central, and this should be natural and rewarding. Children need to have their confidence bolstered, to enjoy the pleasures of language and stories without feeling any anxiety about failure. Parents should not be overburdened by a sense of competition with neighbours' children, or by the desire to push their own as hard as possible. Knowing the different rates of development in children and the complexity of the process, they should not worry. Children will learn in their own way. They will learn the better for enjoying the shared pleasures of play.

Young children's success at reading comes about not from parental pressure but from their response to a world filled with language, and from talking with siblings and friends as well as adults. The knowledge of what orthography is for, the idea of written symbols, arises naturally from the awareness of language. The desire to know is what helps children learn. The activity of reading, shared between parents and children, helps in the most natural way to give children the understanding of its purpose.

It is one of the most significant realizations of our time (some might say belated, others might say obvious) that parents play a central role in the education of children, even if some of them do not wish to. We know the importance of children's early experience of shared activities, and the fact that it makes a difference to all subsequent attainment. The ability to listen is in itself not as important as the sharing of this activity. Parents continue to be important in helping children to read; experiments in many parts of the country all prove how a combination of school and home-based practice, and the involvement of adults other than teachers, significantly improve reading ability. But we should not need any complex research or scheme to encourage parents to play a major role in the development of their children's learning. All the pre-reading skills, and the attitudes towards reading that underpin the whole process, need to be fostered as much in the home as at school.

The concept of reading

The idea of communication through writing is such a subtle concept that it can only be learnt in a complex way, not through simple explanation. Children will learn the idea through recognition of the practice; just as they learn new words through their context. They very rarely ask about the meaning of a word in a story, but try to interpret unfamiliar material in their own way. Following an explanation of the meaning of a word like 'word' is far more difficult than gaining awareness of its meaning through use of it. Children learn the concept of reading through their ability to ask questions and enjoy stories, their ability to carry out instructions or interpret a picture, to retell a story or arrange pictures in a logical sequence, sing a tune or recognize similarities and differences in objects, as they come to recognize them in letters and words. The concept of reading will arise out of the abilities to concentrate and categorize, together with an awareness of the pleasures of stories.

The sharing of stories

Stories are not only a form of entertainment but a child's means of understanding the world. They play a central role in children's development, and the more they are told and read to children, the better. They are also the most obvious means of sharing the pleasures of reading. Children enjoy stories with a repeated punchline; indeed, they like familiar stories to be told again and again. But children do not need to be mere recipients of stories. They can use their own judgement about particular incidents or characters, or guess what will happen next. They prefer to be, in a sense, part of the story, so that they are engaged in some repeated catchphrase. Their love of recognition of the familiar is an extension of their earlier practice in forming syllables; they are seeing the need for structure in stories as well as in sounds.

Stories are also a starting point for other activities: describing what happens in the pictures, predicting what will appear next. The more able children are to describe or relate what they have heard or experienced, the more they will be able to understand stories translated into script. Stories can be a starting point for other uses of language: the use of symbols or signs and the development of rhymes and jingles. Children can also learn to understand sequences in time: consequences and the sense of an ending. Children are so fond of the familiar that they will get to know certain stories so well that they can virtually imitate the skill of reading through their exact memory of the text. From that to understanding the idea of reading is a very short step.

Every reader of a story should be unafraid of conveying all that is possible through tone and gesture. Even the shyest of parents can learn to bring out the best in a story by reviewing it carefully beforehand and gaining a sense of how to stress certain aspects, while freeing enough attention to involve the children listening. In preparing a story it is wise to note which pictures can be shown and when: some because they could invite a comment, and others because they are one way of illustrating what is being read. Any reader can train his or her voice so as to be able to convey excitement and variety. It follows naturally that the conditions in which a story is read are important, and that stories can be read or told at any time, and not just as an emergency time-filler or a reward at the end of the school day.

Part of the importance of stories is that they help children learn to listen, and to concentrate. In school nothing is worse than a struggle against disorder, when more attention is paid to keeping children quiet than to telling the story; it is for this reason that the teacher's convictions are so important. Children also need to be encouraged to ask questions about the story. These questions allow them to engage their own ideas: they may reveal how their minds have made certain associations, and start to tell you something that *seems* irrelevant but to them is part of the story. Stories need to be shared, and not just conveyed, for children's involvement in them is an active one. Children can be asked to tell stories as well as listen to them; although they will seem to give fairly inconsequential plots, or a series of knockabout incidents, they will in fact be practising their sense of sequence and consequence; they will be acknowledging the structures of a story. You could also ask them to retell a story they have just heard, so you can see what kind of choices they make in their narration, and teach them how to reconstruct the events in it. Their interpretation will teach them to find the right words reflectively rather than just spontaneously. Children can be asked to tell stories to each other, either those invented by themselves, or those they have recently heard. For this reason, a whole school class can create a story together, choosing a character and deciding what happens to that character, so they learn to make deliberate choices between different alternatives.

The significance of story

We have been suggesting that part of the importance of reading stories to children is that it enables them to become familiar with the act of reading and the pleasure that can be derived from it. Stories are more important than this. They are ultimately what reading is for. We might not think that 'story' is an apt description of a complex novel, but the word signifies a great deal about the relationship of the self to the rest of the world. Each of us has a 'story' to tell. We deal in telling stories every day. The internalization of experience, giving meaning to events, is 'story'.

Young children come to interpret and understand the world through story. At first stories are like a mirror that reflects their own lives. They like to have simple narratives of their own everyday events. Even at that point, something complex is going on. There is the juxtaposition between the subjective and the objective, between their internal experience and the description from someone else's point of view. Young children realize they are playing a part in other people's lives.

Stories are also the first moment when ordinary everyday reality is transformed into something greater. Every story is to some extent a fantasy. It does not need anthropomorphic creatures like bears and elephants to give the colour of the unreal to ordinary events. Every story reinterprets and suggests a reality outside.

Stories also give a sense of stability. Each person's point of view might be subjective and everything they read may be interpreted idio-syncratically, but stories, once written, remain the same. They can therefore be viewed as a kind of permanent reality, and interpreted personally as such.

Even the most traditional of stories conveys complex layers of meaning. 'Once upon a time.' At once the essence of two kinds of reality are captured. The timelessness of the eternal, the never-changing, and that single moment, that specific event, are juxtaposed. 'Once' is both general and specific. The word invites not only the leap into questions that go beyond the present moment, but recognizes the specific nature of the experience for those about whom the story is told.

And then 'they lived happily ever after'. This favourite ending reminds us of the same thing. 'They lived' in the past and their lives came to an end. At the same time this refers ironically to 'ever after', that impossible longing for eternal bliss. Even while acknowledging the fantasy of the story, we are given a reminder of mutability.

Stories remain the heart of life, as they are of reading.

Part three

The first stages of reading

'And I'll tell you a secret – I can read words of one letter! Isn't *that* grand! However, don't be discouraged. You'll come to it in time.'

(Lewis Carroll, *Through the Looking Glass*, Chapter 9)

Chapter 9
Helping children to read

John has been queuing for ten minutes for his turn to read a page from his graded text. When his turn comes he stumbles over the first, simple word. The teacher has covered all the other clues; the picture, and the other marks on the page. John does not know what to do, or where to look for comfort. Soon all he does is wait for the moment to pass. He does not concentrate more carefully under the teacher's scrutiny. On the contrary, he becomes more flustered by not being able to guess what the teacher wants him to do.

In that typical, and often repeated, scene, the two difficulties of learning to read are encapsulated. One difficulty is that learning to read is a personal as well as complex task. Children need to do it in their own way; just as they learn language through a mixture of discrimination, guessing at context and association, so the task of reading depends upon the way in which they can separate out the necessary clues from all the extraneous material and analyse them. The other difficulty is that being aware of the personal nature of learning does not mean that the teacher does nothing; it just means that what teachers and parents do must be more closely geared to the realities of learning. The concept of 'barking at print', which a routine repetition of well-known meaningless phrases can entail, merely ensures that children associate print with misery. Once they find themselves unable to look for clues, once they show that they do not know how to interpret the signs, it is important to go back to those principles on which reading is based. Merely to try to chase them up the paths of reading schemes will not ensure that they are capable of leading themselves. To diagnose what the problem consists of is far more helpful. And for that we need to be constantly aware of the nature of the reading process, as well as the means by which we can help it.

The following chapters concentrate on the core of the skill of reading, but can only be fully understood in relation to the whole context of reading: the development of language, the development of perception, and understanding the purpose and rewards of reading. The mistakes that children make in reading are nearly always because they have not understood one of the basic processes. A sound preparation for reading is the only sure way of overcoming the mistakes that become ingrained, as in spelling. Children do not learn through a succession of stages according to their age, but often revert to what seems like more atavistic behaviour. To ease their development they should be allowed to revert occasionally to what is simple and comes easily, to what seems to us repetitive but which for them is a kind of internalizing, of making automatic a skill that is still being thought about rather than taken for granted. It is important for us to know the difference between those tasks that extend a child and those that are for consolidating what is already known. Both are necessary.

As children grow older, the minds they bring to bear on the problems of reading will have more experience, but the problems remain the same. This suggests that 'remedial' children do not need to be given separate tasks. The important teaching technique common to all is to vary the approach; to go 'back' to games of visual and auditory perception rather than rub children's noses in their mistakes. Learning depends on the balance between hope and observation, between expectations fulfilled and disappointed, and between right guesses and mistakes, which are part of the daily experience.

The use of symbols

It is sometimes difficult to understand the problems of reading simply because we take it for granted. It is as if we take it for granted that photographs are an accurate representation of the objects portrayed in them, and forget that they are a two-dimensional representation of a complex three-dimensional reality. Learning to read is rather like being able to prise the symbol from its context, understanding that the marks are a means to an end and not an end in themselves. Chinese children, with their logographic system, manage to learn 2000 characters in the first four years of primary school, since the stylized visual representation embodied in a pictogram is in many ways easier to comprehend than the largely arbitrary link between words and meanings. Even English-speaking children sometimes find it easier to understand a different system of writing. In one experiment a group of children learnt a series of Chinese characters after failing to learn to read English syllables.

Children tend to search for a visual analogy between the word and the concept it symbolizes, rather than to convert the symbols on the page into speech, and to make the association from spoken word to meaning. This tendency is sometimes exacerbated by their inclination to see and remember the word as a gestalt visual whole, much as people tend to associate an abstract shape with a concrete analogy. The relationship between sight and sound is always a difficult one until the final union; it is then taken for granted. These difficulties are made more severe by the limitations of the phoneme system, in which one letter can be represented on the page in a variety of ways, and can represent a variety of sounds, so that there is no simple one-to-one correspondence for children to identify. There could not be, in an alphabetic system, a complete correspondence of sight to sound, clearly explicable to children. The very ways in which some small visual differences are significant and others are not shows how complex is the demand on children. Every sound for:

T, t, o, T, t

remains the same; for all the variations of the written code; 'y' and 'y' are the same letter, but 'd' and 'b', which have little more visual difference, are not. Certain symbols are used commonly: £ or $ in place of the alphabetic pound or dollar. Even three and seven are more commonly given in word signs: 3 and 7. Furthermore, English is an illogical system in its manipulation of sounds. 'T' and 'h' together make one sound; but the letter 'x' is in fact, made up of two sounds, '/k'/ and 's'.

Even the simplest analogy between sight and sound needs to be worked out. Sign languages, such as pictograms:

symbolizing fish, or ideograms when the sun:

stands for time, are far easier for children to understand at first. But children need to be able to categorize and make discriminations of shape based on very different analogies, and to understand the differences between cognitive and semantic categories. Since the process of categorizing is so fundamental to learning it does children no harm, throughout the process of learning to read, to sharpen their visual senses and mental abilities by making use of the various ways in which objects (or shapes) can be listed; for example, things which float and things which sink, or different combinations of shape and sequences.

Sight and sound

One of the earliest difficulties for children when they listen to speech is to distinguish one word from another. Every sound seems to blend with the next in such a way that they cannot analyse the separate words, since people when talking do not pause between one word and another. For children the result is, literally, like a foreign language. It is only when they know the words that they can tell when the breaks between the words are supposed to come. The same difficulty can be seen in the analysis of separate words into sounds: it is only through the knowledge of phonemes that such analysis can take place. At least the written language does give some clues, unlike ancient Greek script, which did not allow for any breaks between words. Learning to listen for meaning is a task not unlike that of learning to look at script for significant clues. Most fluent readers take for granted the eye movements on which reading depends. They look at one point in a long word and avoid parts of the text containing short words or punctuation. They learn to scan two or three words at the same time. When children start to read they need to learn to discriminate between single letters and then between larger combinations. Too many eye-movements retard fluency and comprehension. It is important to know where to fixate, to be able to know automatically what to look for. Skilled readers recognize the meaning of more words than are fixated, and probably use the meanings of words ahead of fixation as markers to guide their eye movements in their interpretation of the text.

Many of the skills of reading need to be learnt in such a way that they become a means to an end, and not an end in themselves. While children 'read' from the page in their expressionless way, they are still caught up in the difficulties of script. Once they have mastered the idea of the analogy between sight and sound, they have the means of applying that understanding to different circumstances. Early readers concentrate more narrowly on the text and try to work out carefully a skill that needs use and practice rather than scrutiny.

Reading is not only a matter of making connections between sight and sound, since the correlation is not exact. Reading is the ability to understand the way in which blended sounds make up words, and letter blends make up sounds. It is almost impossible to sound one letter without another. A consonant like 'c' or 'k' cannot be said without the suggested vowel. 'Kugh' and 'tugh' are two of the sounds that make up the word 'cat' but both sounds have to blend with the vowel. The most significant feature of a word is the way in which the letters blend together, whether it is the difference the letter makes at the end of the word – 'hat' and 'hate' – or the digraphs that make up the most significant feature. Children learn to internalize the most distinctive features of words, by understanding not only the letters that make up the word but the way in which they act together to do so. The single letter, as symbol, is not as important as the use to which it is put in context. Fluent readers have learnt to see the significant morphemes even in a word they have not seen before. No readers ever go back to that first stage of having to pick out every letter (unless they are looking at a foreign language that means nothing to them). The main feature of words, and the means for analysing them, is not the single letters but the way they are associated with each other to make up words. It is through blends that the connection between the recognition of letters and the immediate recognition of words is made.

Interventions

While we know that each child learns to read in his or her own way, we know that at the heart of the process is that elusive connection between segments of speech and written symbols. This can, for some, remain a mysterious and impenetrable link. At what point is there an exact correspondence, and when does the whole process become more lubricious? The fluent reader jumps past whole words which make sense, while the slower reader is faced by meaningless segments of symbol.

We know that children have to learn; but there are also means of helping. The first rule is that 'intervention' should not be an impediment. Too often the inability to read is seen as a failure to grasp the most obvious facts: it is failure of a test, an end in itself rather than the unavailability of a skill. Some interventions, such as set reading hours, can actually do more harm than good. Once that is recognized, however, we must concede that it is always possible to help, given the right motivation. Any support is to be welcomed, and any parent or other adult, or, even more, other children, can usefully and creatively be employed as helpers and supporters.

That said, it helps if the helper knows about and is sensitive to the peculiar difficulties of learning to read. While it is helpful to have an audience to read to – patient listeners – it is much more helpful to have someone who knows how to explain and can analyse mistakes. Programmes that involve parents and other adults in the teaching of reading are invariably successful, and successful in proportion to the amount of time given to training the participants. While one characteristic of these programmes is that their methods and evaluations are rarely disseminated, it is clear that they succeed partly because of improved attitudes. They demonstrate what reading is for. They make it clear that there is nothing ultimately impossible about the task.

Intervention programmes that have helped individual children who have difficulties in learning to read have certain features in common (hence this book). One is that they concentrate both on the usefulness of reading, on the outcomes and the experience, and at the same time on the phonological problems. Just going through tests, or listening to failure, is not enough. Merely repeating phonics does not help. It is the subtle blend of the clues and the outcomes that supports the learner. Direct instructions, real teaching, from an unthreatening source, definitely helps. Parents who have time, who help in decoding the text and who regard reading as valuable and enjoyable, prove to be very important.

Such parents are, of course, acting as teachers, engaged with individual children. This is why such intervention programmes are successful. Reading is personal. It is not a matter of imbibing facts on which to be tested, even if it is sometimes reduced to this for the purpose of inspection.

If parents and other adults make good teachers of reading, the same is true of other children. Their exploration of the means to an end can be both sensitive and demanding. We often undervalue and always under-use the potential of pupils to help each other, but pupils can help each other. Learning is then not a competition but an exploration.

Methods of learning to read

There are many approaches to the teaching of reading, some of which, despite their exclusivity, become influential. Some concentrate upon the skills of reading, defined as the response to a series of stimuli. Some depend on the use of experience, seeing reading as one of the four aspects of language, closely linked to children's speech. One model of reading isolates five specific skills of a general kind, including memory, cognition (ie understanding that the word has a meaning), context, structure and evaluation. Another sees reading as a mixture of five domains of comprehension, from the literal, through reorganizational and inferential, to the evaluative and appreciative. They all try to find analogies to illuminate the connections between sight, sound and experience.

These approaches to learning to read all overlap. Concentration on one particular model does not mean that other types of experience must be excluded. In fact, one of the underlying but unstated assumptions in the research on reading is that there is a need for parents and teachers to think carefully about the needs of individual children, in terms of both their linguistic environment, and of sensitivity to their own approaches to reading. In each of the 'models' of reading we see the more general capacities of children being brought to bear. Their memory and their experience, as well as their skills, are all understood to be a central, not a peripheral, part of reading, and the more detailed research confirms this. The main factor in modern approaches to reading is to see it within the context of learning as a whole.

We help children to learn to read not by confronting them with the problem of reading, but by explaining how to find a way through the problem. To do this we need to prepare their ability to think; to be perceptually alert and to be curious to learn. Some fundamental concepts should be made clear at every stage of learning to read. Before we concentrate on the ability to spot the significant clue in reading a word, we must remember that we have to teach children concepts such as 'word', 'sentence' and 'letter'. We often take for granted that children understand every word they are accustomed to hear; it is only when they begin to use words that we can be sure they do. Our teaching is greatly simplified if some obvious technical distinctions are familiar to children. These include 'left' and 'right': 'up' and 'down': 'top' and 'bottom'. The very familiarity with these dimensions reinforces the ability to understand the two-dimensional nature of print. 'Sentence' after all, is not an easy concept to explain, but it is a useful one since it shows a child not only why the words on a page have a significant overall shape, but how they correspond to the concepts we are expressing.

The ability to make sense of categories can be enhanced by explaining the differences between the 'rough' and the 'smooth', the 'light' and the 'heavy', the 'round' and the 'square'. Using some simple materials like beads or cubes we can concentrate on concepts like 'left' and 'right', on 'smaller' or 'bigger', on the 'same' or 'different'. We can use ribbons to teach concepts such as 'short' and 'long', 'shorter' and 'longer'. We can even go further and divide pictures or objects into more abstract distinctions such as that between 'work' and 'play' or 'beautiful' and 'ugly'. Children can be asked to think of as many examples as they can to fit into categories such as 'towns', 'cars', or 'names'. They can also play simple versions of 'twenty questions'.

One of the most significant concepts for children to learn is the correspondence between two different things. This can greatly be helped by learning to count and match. One of our earlier manoeuvres should be to teach fundamental numeracy, up to the level where the vocabulary of simple arithmetic makes sense. Even singing games like 'three blind mice' or 'ten green bottles' are a starting point for the ability to use numbers, which is itself a way of categorizing objects. We can reinforce the ability to understand concepts by teaching children to recognize certain symbols, whether we invent them ourselves or point them out on packets or hoardings. The very ability to translate a simple shape

into a face or a car shows the capacity children have to see symbols rather than the original objects reduced to their basic components. The teaching of cartoon-like drawing is one of the means of developing their ability to communicate through visual expression. No one ever suggested that a tree looks like this:

And yet it has become as much a symbol as a true representation.

One of the correspondences of one thing to another concerns sounds in relation to symbols. This is best illustrated in the problem of the alphabet: whether we should teach it, and if so, when. We know that there is no relationship between the names of the letters and their sounds; it is merely a different nomenclature used for distinct purposes. Thus we need not worry about the alphabet until the child has grasped the basic idea of the blending of letters. It is only after the ability to put sounds into meaningful wholes has been developed that we need to describe the conventions of an alphabet. Until this happens it is sometimes useful to invent names for letters that are close to their normal use: such as 'te' or 'na'. Afterwards we can show what we 'call' them, starting with the simpler names, like 'A', 'B', but leaving more difficult ones like 'C' (where the alphabet word contrasts with the sound of the letter) until later. When the alphabet is being taught, it is wise to teach lower and upper case at the same time. Children can learn the different graphemes by putting cards together, like this:

A	B	C	D	E
a	b	c	d	e

They can learn the names of the letters at the same time. This can be done the moment children are familiar with nearly all the letters they would normally use. The reason one should not wait too long before teaching the alphabet is partly because it is inevitable that children will come across it anyway at home and elsewhere, and partly because of the importance of learning the order of the alphabet (since using every index, as well as every dictionary, requires knowledge of it).

Children learn to read in their first moments of play. We should never be afraid of retracing some of those first steps in learning. Their attempts to make sense of the world, by organizing their own perceptions, and their involvement in their own experience, are all part of a process that does not come to an end. The fundamentals of learning, as well as the characteristics of behaviour and attitude, remain the same. Once children see the concepts that underlie reading, as well as its purpose, they will quite suddenly grasp the means of making sense of it, and use it as a means of making more sense of their exploration of the world.

Chapter 10
Letters

The relationship between the letters on the page and the sounds they represent is not always a consistent one. Many letters, like 'a', can stand for several sounds; other letters –such as 'c' and 'k' – can sound the same. The series of 'phonemes' that makes up the sounds of a language is a set of agreed signals of meaning. It does not cover all the sounds possible in a language, which is why each language has a different range of 'phonemes', but within a fairly wide range of accents there is enough agreement about the symbols to make us intelligible to each other. Children can easily understand the different pronunciations of words; they hear the symbolic meaning of the word despite the wide range of actual sounds used to pronounce it. The same acceptance of symbolic value is seen in the way that a 'grapheme' can be understood despite the variety of ways in which it can be written.

Despite the lack of immediate correspondence between sight and sound, children clearly need to learn to recognize particular letters so that they can understand how they relate to one another. It is easy to say that a child needs to learn the exact correspondences, but this is difficult in practice because the relationship between sight and sound is rarely static, and depends as much on blending two or more shapes and sounds together as on seeing which sound to choose when the visual clue is given. Children do not learn just through the 'simple' process of being able to add one sound to one shape until they follow all the variations of the alphabet. The abilities to learn by guessing, and associating a number of correct guesses, and by associating a series of sentences with the words written in a story book, are examples of the child's varied styles of learning. The ability to understand 'phonemes' and 'graphemes' is a question not just of teaching simple phonic drills (many children have failed to read under this regime) but of explaining the principles on which the alphabet method of writing language works. The difficulty for teachers lies in correlating the perception of laterality, or matching block designs, to the perception of the printed words.

Children have a different way from adults of discriminating between pairs of letters. Whereas adults consistently start discriminating by separating sharp letters from diagonal ones, 'm' from 'c', and then simple rounded letters like 'c' from 'p', children of seven start to discriminate between letter shapes by splitting simple curves from straight lines: for example, 'p' from 'm'. Children see letters like 'e', 'f', 'm', 'n' and 'w' as being similar, whereas adults see 'c', 'g', 'e', 'p', 'f' and 'r' as similar. Children tend to confuse letters in ways that seem unexpected to us. But then primary school children's ability to recall aural information, unlike that of adults, is actually better than their ability to recall visual information. To help them to become fluent in associations, children need to be helped in a variety of ways: not through a repeated insistence on particular clues, but through a series of games, in which they can use and demonstrate their ability. Many children subconsciously use mnemonics like rhymes or pictures in learning to distinguish between letters, and many teachers use similar devices.

Phonemes

One of the easiest ways to develop a child's sense of the distinct sounds that make up the overall sound of a word is through rhyme. The learning of simple rhymes, and the inventing of phrases made up of similar-sounding words, are both effective. Children can also be asked to complete a sentence with a word that rhymes with one they have been given, for example, 'He has just come in; he looks so . . .' This ability to think of a rhyme in a semantic framework, combining different styles of thought, can be encouraged by suggesting a series of clues for a word of the right sound. For instance, we can ask what colour rhymes with 'shed' or 'back' or 'glue'. Children can also be asked to discriminate between words that rhyme and those that do not; the difference between pairs like 'bin/ben' and 'bark/mark'.

Rhyme is a fairly simple way of communicating the concept of the sounds of vowels. But vowels cannot be learnt without the accompanying consonants. So it is not practicable (or desirable) to teach either vowels or consonants in isolation. Teaching vowels by themselves is like trying to teach the different uses of an 'anonymous' sound like that of the 'e' in 'the'. The main advantage of teaching sounds in terms of rhyme is that it draws attention to the middle of words rather than just the beginnings. The traditional link of 'a' with apple, or 's' with sun does not necessarily lead the child to understand the same letter in a different position. It is worth teaching the sounds of letters in the middle, or the end, as well as at the beginning of words.

One of the most effective ways of teaching phonemes is the most obvious: through showing a series of pictures (say of a house or a dog) and asking which of these starts with the sound 'd(o)'. The teacher can half sound the 'o' or other vowel (it is better that than to say 'd-uh'). Children can be asked to think of all the words that start with the same sound, or they can play a game of 'I spy'. But whatever device is used, it is better in the long run to take an initial consonant together with a vowel, rather than isolate the vowel. It is also useful for children to guess the sound of a letter when they have a visual clue. To enhance this sense of the use of words we can, in teaching a sound like 'b', go beyond asking for a list of words by asking children what they can do with it, for example 'buy' or 'bite', or where they can find it. The same techniques can be varied by asking children to think of things to eat or drink; anything that makes them think at the same time not only of the particular sound that begins a word, but also of the use of the word or its classification.

At various times a teacher can use the blackboard or a card with just one letter on it, indicating its place as part of a word and asking children to say whether it stands for 'dog' or 'bull'. The teacher can also read out a sentence like 'Every morning we let out the b . . .' so that the clue of the first letter is allied to the context; it becomes another way of discovering the answer. Children should in fact be given a semantic clue as well as the bare letter; for they learn by a blending of associations and contextual clues.

The ability to recognize and place the sounds of particular letters should not be confined to the beginnings of words. If children know the letter and sound 'a' they should learn to recognize it within words like 'black' or 'match'. Attention can be drawn to the letter by the use of colours to highlight the relevant parts of words. When children are able to distinguish two letters and sounds, and can recognize them easily, it is worth reading out a sentence in which one particular sound comes up several times. Children then count the 'appearance' of the letter: this can most easily be done by giving them a single choice between two letters they are learning to distinguish.

Children can also play simple games with each other to make them fluent in their associations of letters and words. One child has a card with a picture of a sun on one side and 's' on the other. Given a range of cards of this kind, two children can play opposite each other and say what the letter stands for. A variation of this game is one which makes use of a large card with several pictures on one side, letters on the other, and a series of 'portholes' connecting the letters and pictures. On being asked which letter begins the name for a picture, the child (who will in this instance be looking at the letter side of the card) places a pencil in the appropriate porthole. Children can also be given several letter cards: when a particular word comes up they choose a card to match it. The teacher can also aid recognition of letters by writing up a series of words, or spelling a series of words that begin with either of two letters that are being taught. Children then put the initial letters in the order of the words, like 'sun' 'tap' and 'saw'. This can be a technique used with the last letter of a word, as well, as in 'put', or in using both letters as in 'sat'. A variation on this is to ask the children to put the letter into the right space: to ask, in a word like 'cat', where the 't' goes out of the three possible places, beginning, middle and end. The children learn not only the sound/shape correspondence but its relationship to a whole word, and to the sequence of letters.

Graphemes

The learning of individual phonemes and individual letters is a central element in developing the ability to read, even if it is not necessarily the first element to be learnt. It also symbolizes the difficulties of the whole process, since the recognition of individual letters depends on being able to focus on particular things that carry meaning. Having learnt to make sense out of their perceptual world, having understood perspective and distance, children need to focus on the significance of *one* shape, seen from a particular direction, whatever its size.

While learning the segments of sounds that make up words, children need to understand the visual consistency of the same recurring shape. A teacher can ask children to recognize a letter like 's' when it appears in a sequence such as 's s a s s r', or else continue a particular sequence of 'shapes' such as 'a a b a a b a a ...', etc. The development of left to right orientation, and the extension of visual perception, are applied to the recognition of the shape of letters. Even if the teacher concentrates on a particular sequence that a child has already learnt, this 'patterning' can be a useful way of making sure that the child is familiar with all the shapes that make up our alphabet. Many of the techniques that can be used to help children recognize and discriminate between shapes are also devices that help them make essential visual distinctions even before they approach letters.

Just as it is tempting to assume that children learn in a series of stages, it is tempting to devise a fixed order for the teaching of various letters. No fixed routine is sacrosanct but, it is important to remember a few basic rules that might prevent confusion. It is better to avoid letters that sound too similar – that come within the same phonetic group – like 'p' and 'b'. It is better to have contrasts, as between 'p' and 'm', or 'f' and 'l'. It is also preferable to avoid presenting letters that look similar, such as 'b' and 'd': a confusion, or possible confusion, can be saved for later, when it can be dealt with through the use of mnemonics, as in:

(dog) and (bear)

The most useful rule for the learning of individual letters is to present children with a mixture of vowels and consonants. If teachers begin by comparing 't' and 's' and then go on to include 'i', they can make sure that the children know these three letters perfectly. Another reason for choosing these three is the possibility they give of making up words like 'it' and 'sit'.

The technique of taking two consonants and one vowel, so that simple words can be made up from the start, combines the use of two skills, association and the recognition of whole words. The concentration upon clearly differentiated units of words means that the blending of digraphs takes place from the beginning. After learning the three letters 't', 'i', and 's', children can go on to learn a clear sequence of letters such as 'l', 'c' and 'a'; then 'f', 'm' and 'e'; then 'b', 'w' and 'o'; then 'h', 'r' and 'u', until they have a set of letters out of which simple words can be put together.

There are many techniques a teacher can use to make children familiar with different letter shapes. The ability to be able to discriminate confidently and quickly is important for children, since they need to be able to grasp the symbolic 'value' in each letter, especially in relation to other letters. This is an archetype of all kinds of learning where the abilities to discriminate, make quick judgements, remember and categorize, remain essential. For this reason it is important that children should be encouraged to guess, for that shows that they see the idea. There are no dreadful 'errors' when a child is trying to predict the understanding of the code we share.

One of the simplest techniques is for a child to reproduce certain shapes from memory. This could begin with the simplest of letters, 'o' or 's', and then continue to the more complex, so that at least children for a time retain in their minds the pattern of a shape like 'd'. The teacher can write a series of letters up on a board and then, while the children are not looking, rub one out, to test whether they can remember which one is missing. The letters can be placed on a table and covered up; the children then try to see if there is one missing, as in 'Kim's game'.

Another way of helping children to become familiar with letters is to let them copy the shapes. Tracing or copying gives children practice in their tactile abilities and gives the teacher an opportunity to discuss the concepts of two dimensions and of writing. Learning to read and write at the same time is of immense benefit not only to the child but to the teacher, for both can be sure that the letter shapes are really understood and can actually be used, as well as merely responded to. Pictorial alphabets can also be useful, either ready-made or, better still, made up by the child, so that the letter 'S' is associated with a snake or an 'L' with a ladder.

One of the skills in letter recognition is for children to remember those they know even when they are embedded in many others. If they have the confidence to pick those out, then they have already learnt how to discriminate and how to pay attention to particular clues. It is useful to write names down, out of which children pick the letters that they know and recognize. The same technique can be used with clearly printed materials from a magazine or book. This helps children become familiar with the use of reading; it relates to the experience they have had of seeing people carry out the strange ritual of turning over pages very slowly. Thus children need to learn two essential things: to recognize a particular shape out of many, and to remember what the shape was even if the teacher merely shows a letter to them for a short time and then asks them to reproduce it.

The ability to see the connection between letter shapes can be greatly helped by a series of games where the children need merely to spot the correlations. At first a child needs merely to draw lines from one letter to another, to link those that are the same:

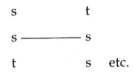

This task can be made more complex by simply making the correspondences diagonal rather than horizontal:

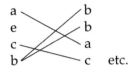

Later, this technique can be used with single letters and the beginnings of whole words:

s ————— sun
t   sun
s   tug   etc.

These discrimination games can be played with numbers as well. It can be a good idea to teach numbers and letters at the same time, because of the similarity in the need for recognition, and also because of the contrast in the concept. The concept of number can be easier to grasp than reading, because the symbols are not as variable, or put to as many uses, as letters.

At one stage children will need to learn the shape of letters in relation to a horizontal line. This can be done through joining up cards:

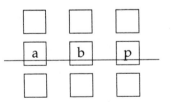

The basic association of letters and sounds can be fostered by asking children to join single letters and pictures of an object whose name begins with the letter being taught.

Writing letters

One of the most useful ways of familiarizing children with letter shapes is to enable them to write them. Children learn language not just by listening to it but by recreating it themselves. Children can be encouraged to use a pencil early, as well as crayons, , to extend their manipulative skills in the shaping of letters. Their love of trying to write and draw, first shown in scribbles, can be used in the extension of their skills in writing. They learn then the concept of individual letters, as well as spacing and blending. Their earliest practice of writing can take place at the same time as letter recognition. They can make up their own letter cards. The ability to manipulate a pencil in drawing can be used to help them copy letter shapes, learning how to hold the pencil, how to rest their hands, and how to recognize what they see well enough to be able to reproduce it.

Some of the earliest exercises in writing should concentrate on the simple basic shapes. The important point to stress is that the two-dimensional differences of each letter are significant. The ability to write depends not only on forming the correct letters but on forming them in the correct manner. Thus children need to practise the shape 'o' by forming it in the way they will be required to do so in order to write:

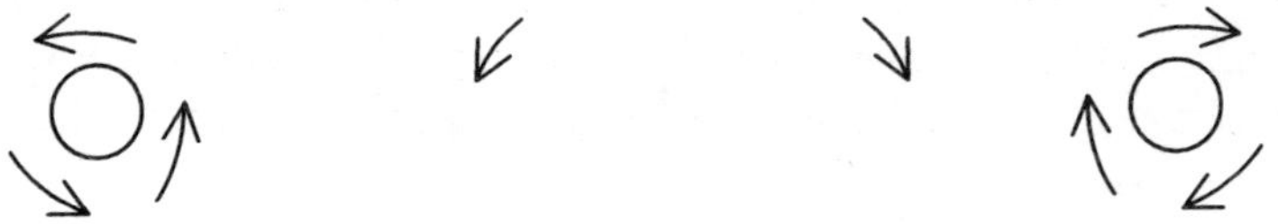

as in 'boy'; the first rather than the second.

When children trace letters they are learning the rhythm that underlies script, and are becoming accustomed to the natural movements downwards, left to right, and the combination of the two:

They also learn the skill of re-tracing the same part of the letter, in order to move onwards smoothly, as in:

We can ask them to trace letters, or follow shapes, or join the dots, always insisting on a certain direction to follow:

This tactile sense will, in fact, help children to recognize the letters more easily.

Special attention can be given to the ease of writing repeated 'c's' as this tends to be one of the more difficult letters:

CCCCC   CCCCCC

The patterns suggested so far demand close observation and control over the pencil.

Writing underlines the skill of visual accuracy. As children become more sophisticated in their ability to reproduce these graphemes, we can ask them to carry out more complicated writing tasks, to develop their ease and fluency as well as their accuracy in the production of letters, for example:

abbaabbaabba

or more complicated doodles:

Once children are able to follow or trace letter shapes we can concentrate on their ability to reproduce those letters they are learning to recognize. We can start with simple script that looks like print, but with no rounded letters. We can then go on to letters formed without the pencil leaving the paper. This is to insist on the most satisfactory way both of writing and recognizing individual letters. So we need to reiterate the use of the basic movements first:

and then begin to explore some of the developments. For each of these there is the sensible conventional way of carrying it out:

↓b↓ ↓h↓ ↓M ↓S↓

At first we naturally concentrate on lower case, although there is no urgent need to insist upon it. Nor is the size of the letters important, as long as there is not too much exaggerated discrepancy between one and another in the same line. It has sometimes been suggested that there should be a rigid sequence in which children learn to write letters, but the problem with sticking to such a sequence is partly that it is too easy to lose the close relationship with reading matter, and partly that children learn by seeing the distinctions between one letter shape and another. The very contrast between writing one letter and another helps children read. It is, however, useful to be aware of certain rules by which the writing of letters can be classified:

those with down strokes	f	l	i	
those with down strokes and swings	b	p	h	r
the anticlockwise curve	c	a	d	g	o
diagonal lines	v	w	y	

One useful concomitant to teaching writing at the same time as reading is the reinforcement of the concept of spaces between words. In putting together their own words children can learn to leave the space of one letter between each pair.

Chapter 11
Letter blends

To make sense of the world we need to be able to analyse its constituent parts, to perceive it in smaller, more manageable sections. We need to learn this because the amount of information we receive is otherwise so great that we would not know how to deal with it. Once we know *how* to classify we also need to know how to build up parts into a whole. When sentences are spoken they do not actually come out in separate words; it is our understanding of the words that helps us analyse what takes place. When we read a line of print we do not go through every letter; we can scan a whole line so fast that we forget the labour of memory and synthesis that once went into reading. A reader who looks at:

axsentencexthatxcontinuesxinxthisxwayxwithxthexspacesxfilled

reads as slowly as an early reader habitually reads.

If English writing were more like the Chinese or Japanese systems one could envisage clear sequences, of memory and exact correspondence of sight and meaning. Blending is such a crucial step in reading, at any level, that it dominates the whole process. Many of the difficulties that children have with reading come about because this central stage is ignored: as if either separate phonics *or* whole words were the two significant factors of reading. Blends need to be emphasized in *all* the early stages of reading, because they are in fact the heart of written script and the heart of meaning, in morphemes. Children see that both syllables of sound and units of meaning are made up by blends of letters. This is something they discover in their own way, in a manner that no psychologist has fully been able to analyse. There are no perfect sequences for learning, since children do not learn by taking in all that is presented to them.

Syllables

Although it is possible to analyse spoken language into phonemes, it is very difficult to produce a consonant without implying a vowel. When the sounds of spoken language are analysed on a spectogram, which tabulates the sound of a voice as it pronounces words, it is clear that in the acoustic sense it is impossible to distinguish a sound like 'd' without including a following vowel, however refined the attempt to capture just the initial sound. Although distinct when written, the consonant does not exist distinctly in terms of sound. The initial consonant automatically becomes part of a syllable. This is one reason why there are so many recurring vowel–consonant patterns, like 'in', 'on', 'un', 'an', 'er' and 'ab'. It has even been suggested that the teaching of reading should be based entirely on the division of words into syllables, concentrating on the main syllabic 'signals'.

All speech is syllabic, with natural phonological contrasts between consonant and vowel. The most important fact about words is that they can be broken into units. Out of the mass of letters, children learn to see that they can be analysed into distinct sections. The difficulty is knowing which sections are complete in themselves, and which letters to ignore. A word like 'television' contains not only the rule of consonant and syllable, in the combinations 'te' and 'le', but a different unit of letters: 'ion'. A word like 'chocolate' contains three different types of combination in 'choc', 'co' and 'late'. Some words, such as 'rhythmic', contain many more letters than syllables.

Spoken words can fairly easily be broken into syllables; the same ability in reading needs to be fostered by an understanding of the different *possible* blends. There are too many syllables for a child to learn them all, but there are certain common rules, like the blending of consonant and vowel, that make it possible to approach an analysis of more difficult parts of words. Children need to understand the two types of syllable: the closed, for example 'hat' and 'hate', which both sound a consonant at the end, and the open, for example 'go', with a vowel sound at the end.

Children learn to make sense of the way in which words are written when they learn that they are made up of a limited number of units combined in different ways. Just as children learn to segment sentences into words, so they need to see how phonemes, the experiments in plausible sound, become syllables to make up words. Fortunately children have an ear for the structure of words, playing with words and disguising them by the addition and manipulation of syllables.

Morphemes

The smallest elements of meaning that make up a word can be either single letters, like the plural 's', or syllables. Some words are obviously packages of morphemes, for example:

In/ter/organ/ize/at/ion/al

Some words can be used as a basis for all kinds of meaning: act, actor, acts, actress, acting, transact, action, interact. The place such syllables play in the English language has even led some researchers to suggest that an understanding of the rules of morphology should be at the basis of learning to read, and that an experiment in changing the phonemic system, such as ita, was bound to fail since it ignored morphemic relationships. What is certain is the fact that there are morphemes, like the past tense '-ed', that children learn in terms of rules in their speech, even applying the rule where it does not apply, and that children can usefully translate this rule to their reading. Even more certain is that children need to learn the syllables that make up words, to look for the constituent parts, whether 'bound', as in un/treat/ed', or a combination of 'free' morphemes, as in 'when/ever'.

The ability to look at syllables rather than either whole words or graphemes is made more important by the fact that children become aware of the way in which words are put together. They generally find the end of words more difficult than the beginnings; that is where most errors occur. The realization that vowels are embedded in syllables helps them translate the awareness of speech into the patterns of a text.

Digraphs

When very young children first learn how to use words, they are discovering how words are made up, learning how to distinguish between significant and insignificant sounds. They are learning the meaning of a syllable, the basic distinction between one 'whole' sound and another. When children learn how to blend letters into a part of a word, or into a whole word, they are making just such a significant breakthrough. Without an understanding of the syllables of a word it is impossible to develop speech, and impossible to understand how we write it down.

The analogy between this 'stage' in learning to read, and the initial learning of speech, is drawn because we must often remind ourselves how important language development remains throughout the process of reading. Children need to understand not only the reason for reading, and to develop a positive attitude towards it, but also to be constantly interested in using language, in expressing themselves and finding new means to do so. As they increase their vocabulary they are able to make more subtle discriminations between sounds and their uses; they see how many new words can be made from the 'rules' embedded in those words and syllables they have already learnt.

While children's understanding of words is continually aided by an encouragement to use them, their appreciation of the way words are made up is supported by the continuing development of their visual and auditory perception. The very continuation of the process of 'reading' pictures, and listening to different sounds, gives children the confidence that underlies their ability to read. If reading is made to seem like a natural part of learning, and if it is related to their other activities, children will be motivated more easily.

One of the reasons for stressing the importance of visual skills is that any blending depends on the ability to overcome reversals, an ability to follow the right visual sequence. The learning of blends will itself help avoid the tendency of some children to make substitutions, but the ability to look closely at visual clues is paramount, and more easily developed in blends than in single letters. Just as children will have learnt to discriminate between the shape of different letters, they can learn to pick out differences in single-syllable words, whether these depend on a single letter, as in sun – sun – sup – sun, or on more, as in mat – mat – mug - mat.

Teachers draw attention to the parts of a word by asking children to say which make it sound different from another one, for example the difference between 'rat' and 'sat' or between 'well' and 'wet'. Children can then learn to pick out similarities and differences in words, whether or not they have an initial consonant. They can, for example, be asked which of these words are the same, whether or not they begin with a 't':

tin   in   an   tin   in

If each syllable is given a particular number, for example 1 = in, 2 = an, children can be asked to put the appropriate number beside a succession of words:

bin   din   dan   tan

They should also be asked to point out the difference between the sounds of words like 'sat' and 'sit' without being told exactly what to listen for. They can be asked to synthesize given parts of a word into a whole, as in the joining of 'ba' and 'at' into 'bat'.

The discrimination of initial digraphs can be helped by a version of 'hide and seek', where children spot the repeated sound in a sentence such as 'Bring me the brush'. They can be asked which words start or end with the same sound in a list of words, such as, in this list:

stay   boat   stocking   train

and asked which words start with the same sound as 'star'?

Children can also be asked to complete a sentence with words that begin with one of two digraphs, such as 'th' and sh', as in 'After you have come in, the door must be –', or 'She was second and he was . . .'.

The teaching of initial consonant digraphs needs to take into account the difference between the two types of 'th', as in 'three' and 'there'. It is better to teach these separately before extending the ability to recognize their different pronunciations.

Children often have difficulty in discriminating between pairs of letters when these are embedded within words. For this reason, it is a most helpful task to get them to recognize digraphs when they are given a series of words like:

mice   match   meat   stop   leaf

where they are to spot each recurrence of 'ea'. Not only will they learn to look for a significant clue, but they might be able to recognize these words after a time. If you ask children to carry out a particular task, it does not mean that they will not go beyond it.

Once children have learnt to discriminate between different parts of words, it is easier for them to recognize simple one-syllable words that at first look alike. They can circle words that are alike from a list such as:

mug   tug   tup

106

and the teacher can vary the task by asking them to concentrate on the beginning, end or middle. Once children have learned to spot a distinct blend or pair of letters, as in 'ar', they can be encouraged to make different kinds of words out of them. Having learnt to recognize a blend, they can proceed to synthesize what they have learnt into new forms. The letters 'ar', for instance, can be made into words as different as 'part', 'art' and 'car'. By learning to spot the particular letters, children will more naturally look for the other distinct clues (and therefore blends) that make up new words.

The distinction between a digraph and a word is a very fine one. This is to our advantage in teaching. At no time is it particularly necessary to concentrate purely on single letters, or, indeed, on such a narrow correspondence between a letter and a sound that the words we use every day do not enter into the process. Concentration on parts of a word not only covers the important element of blending, but inevitably carries over into both the recognition and the analysis of simple words. Thus children can soon learn to discriminate between, and say, pairs of words like 'sun' and 'tug'. When children know the value of a digraph such as 'ed', they can soon learn how to add a prefix so that it has a meaning. For this purpose the teacher can use a simple 'roulette wheel' on which the digraph is static, and a series of letters revolve around until they are placed next to it to make up a word:

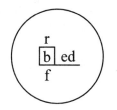

This can be varied with a number of digraphs. Alternatively, children can be asked to convert one word into another, either simply, by changing the same part of a word every time:

tin	into	tan
din	into	dan

or else by alternating the change of one part of the word and the other:

tin	into	bin	
bin	into	pin	etc.

It is always useful to put reading into the context of a wider policy; even the simplest phonic clues can be made more interesting. If children are told a sentence such as 'He has a hat', they should be able to 'read' the right word on being given 'She is f...'. They work by analogy, by seeing the combination of context and common sense, and by the transfer of a simple clue: a style of learning that is true of most children's experiences. Given two sentences of the above kind, children can also be asked to point out which words are similar. Games that consolidate what they already know, and give them confidence and the speed of reaction that comes with confidence, remain useful all the time.

For the blending of final consonants simple cards with clues can be made, for example:

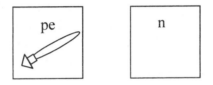

The picture could be split into two so that there is also a 'jigsaw' effect. But the ending of words needs particular attention as well as the beginning. If enough practice in blending has generally taken place, this should not prove too difficult.

One of the difficulties of reading arises because there is no exact correspondence between sight and sound. There are too many phonic rules to be useful; children need to adapt to circumstances in which the art of reading is based on an idea that is imprecise and constantly changing. The only way to use this fact is to show from the beginning how every letter changes according to its position. For this reason alone the stress on digraphs is important; each letter has a value in itself, but is really only significant in coding information when it is placed next to another letter. It is through an understanding of blends and syllables that children inwardly digest the peculiar significance of reading.

It is best to start by concentrating on easier digraphs such as 'sh', 'st', 'ch', 'sp' and 'wh'. This learning can be helped by relating a particular digraph to different pictures that illustrate it, such as a chair and a chain to illustrate 'ch'. Once there is a strong sense of rhyme, the fact that the same sound can be spelt in many different ways, for example:

he   see   tea

is no longer such a frightening barrier to a child's grasp of reading.

Blends and words

If children have concentrated on blending digraphs, they will already have learnt the ability to decode words. The ability to analyse will mean children are not confined to a few key words, but are able to apply their knowledge to new areas. They will then make sense of much longer words, by knowing how to recognize the syllables that make them up, a process that can be encouraged by drawing their attention to longer words with which they are familiar.

To begin with, we wish to make sure they can easily read new simple words. If we have observed the sequence of concentrating on letters at the beginning of a word and then at the end, at the same time as revealing the digraphs 'ba – at', then the next stage will be comparatively easy, when we use ostensibly more complex words like 'st -- op'. The main ability is that of making new words out of simple phonic bases; note that the emphasis is on the child's building of words, and not merely on the reception of a recognizable 'given' word. Thus with a base like 'ad', the child can make 'bad', 'sad', and longer words thereafter.

While children are constructing new words, and reminding themselves of the bases on which words are built, they can be reminded of the synthesizing of syllables into longer words by being presented with the parts of a word like fi/sh/er/man, out of which they say the word as a whole. They do not need to be able to 'read' the whole word at this stage, but to know what it consists of.

As a reminder of what they have already done, as well as a slight extension, children can be asked to find the words that are alike except for the first letter in a sequence like 'fake', 'sake', 'cook', 'take', 'fade' and 'rake', so that even those who do not 'read' the words fast can, by looking carefully, see where the differences lie, and through increasing familiarity, 'read' the whole words quickly after a time. Children can also be asked to put cards with whole words on them into piles according to the way they end, such as with a 'd', 'l' or 's', as in 'mud' or 'bull'. Once again, the words themselves can be discussed, even while the children are looking for clues that are just part of them. To underline exact discrimination, children can be given a series of cards with words that are similar to each other, such as 'pig/peg', 'car/cat' and 'leg/log'; they place the right card against pictures of some of the objects.

The first stages

Many simple games are based on children's ability to make new words out of given syllables, the ability to substitute one letter for another so that a new word emerges. Children enjoy 'inventing' new words within the phonemic structure of English, as well as seeing how far their vocabulary runs. It is for this reason that the game of making a series of substitutions, sometimes of the first letter, and sometimes of the last, is useful. Children can, for example, be asked to make a list converting 'cat' to 'bat', to 'bag', 'bad', 'had' and 'has', and see how far they can extend it. They should be encouraged to use the words in spoken sentences. It is also useful to use as many games as possible that extend the fluency of children's manipulation of words. The game of 'snap' can be adapted to allow children to make words out of distinct blends, when one child has one half of a card:

and another child has the other half:

Children can also play games with cards that have either single letters or digraphs written on them, for example:

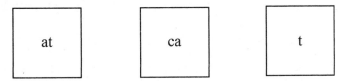

They then put these together to make as many sets as possible. Just like adults playing 'Scrabble', children are apt to think of words that do not actually exist. They will not let each other get away with mere invention.

Games using the principle of blending parts into a whole, when a series of syllables is given on cards, can be extended in a number of ways, from using fairly simple words, with clues (that is, pictures can be added):

110

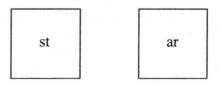

to quite long words which children come across for the first time.

Learning which combinations of letters make up words, and which do not, prevents children from hoping that merely looking at the script will be enough. When children are working by themselves, they need to be sure which words do exist, and which do not; which syllables match, and which do not. If they see how many words can be made around a central digraph such as 'ar', as on a simple slide, it is as important for them to see which words cannot be made as which can.

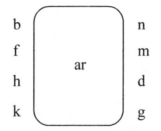

The ability to pick out a sound that is part of a word can be helped by giving the child a series of cards with words on them, concentrating on particular digraphs, especially if the child has experienced difficulties with them. The children can be given cards with digraphs on them, as in words like 'train' and 'near', and asked to pick out the appropriate sound in a sentence or look for the particular digraph in a book. To make sure that the combination of sound and sense is stressed the teacher can ask simple riddles, such as 'I am round', 'You eat off me', or 'I start with the same sound as please . . .'. Sometimes the auditory clue can come first.

A number of word-building games are commercially available, but teachers, if they have time, can make them. Cards which fit together like a very simple jigsaw, on which different parts of the same word are written, can demonstrate very simply the different ways in which words can be blended. Thus on one card we would find:

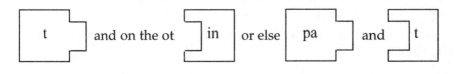

The first stages

Children can 'build walls' out of a succession of simple words, when they are give a series to start from;

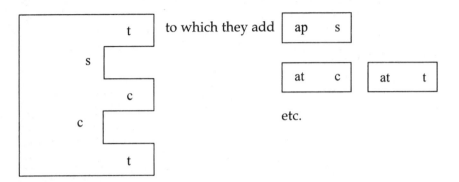

until they have made a coherent succession of short words.

Even for those who worry about the inculcation of bad habits, 'bingo' is a useful game for making children familiar with single words. Children are given a card with a series of words that they must cover up when the matching word is picked. The words used can vary from simple ones, like 'tap', 'cat', 'fun' and 'sun' to the more complex. One particular difficulty can be used as a starting point, for example:

sack	cake	shake
black	slack	rack
sake	bake	take

While children are learning to recognize simple words they can also be learning to fill in the missing vowels from longer words, such as:

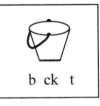

b ck t

Children can fill in missing parts of simple questions by thinking of particular digraphs that would fit, as in 'Do .. ops sell ... ps?' (They can then be asked to answer the question.) The ability to understand the basis of so many words can be emphasized again by asking children

112

to make up word families based on syllables such as 'ail' or 'ain', for example nail, sail, tail, train, chain and rain. One game that enables children to think of answers while using their knowledge of reading consists of giving a clue, and making the answer consist of either of two alternatives. If the question is 'This – has ears', the answer can be either 't–' or '–t'. Children again need to think and look for the visual clue.

Children's ability to understand how words are built can be enhanced by the blending of single letters with larger parts, as in the linking of words like 'lack' and 'lame' with 'b' to make new words, or, indeed, with the adding of an 's' to make a plural, for that is itself a blend. Children can also be asked to choose whether a letter can, or cannot, be added to words like 'see' or 'bee', and if so, which letters can be added. To draw attention to the middle of words children can be asked simply to match those which are similar, for example out of:

ear	smell
nose	hear
mouth	eat

Card games blending parts of words can also concentrate on important prefixes and suffixes that apply to so many longer words, as in 'un', 'dis', 'pre' or 'tion'.

Chapter 12
Word building

Words are usually thought of as the most significant units of meaning, although it is only in a sentence that thoughts can be expressed. Words are only labels in comparison. The first thoughts of a child need to be expressed in single words – 'I have to use words when I'm talking to you' – and words are the more significant as they extend their vocabulary.

The awareness of words and the development of their use, run in parallel with the development of reading. The skill of reading assumes the awareness of words as separate entities. It is, for example, difficult to read a sentence in which the separate words are not clearly spaced, such as:

Heisinthekitchendoingthewashingup

It is also important to remember that we find it easy to read while not 'seeing' particular words. There are many examples where an extra word is automatically ignored, for example:

Please keep off
off the grass

Larger sentences make the unnecessary extra harder to detect.

Fluent readers read differently. They find it easy to read something that looks as if it has a particular order, even if it does not make sense, than a series of obviously disconnected words. Thus:

When we came to go out in to laugh wildly and squash the cat can be read fast. Being confronted by:

Circumspect only fishing probity full going normality

jolts the reader into the position of contemplating each word in isolation.

There are ostensibly two different techniques for understanding the structure of words. The 'analytical' approach is to break down the word into its component parts, including each morpheme. Alternatively, the word can be 'synthetically' constructed from the component syllables, built up into the whole. For children there are no great differences between the two approaches. If they are aware of the ways in which words are made up, if they understand the blends and the syllables, they will also be aware of how to approach a new word, and see the consistent 'habits' of construction. Whether children make sophisticated guesses or base judgements on defined criteria, the analysis of what is known and the ability to make judgements on the unfamiliar are both important.

There are always two possible approaches to the reading of new words, that of looking for the visual information that presents itself in the features of the word, and that of recognizing the sequences of a word based on the knowledge of how words are constructed. The two techniques ultimately blend, but they do so because the fluent reader scans all words in a similar way, blending the recognition of the familiar with the analysis of the new. For this reason it is sometimes difficult for children to make progress in reading at that stage when they rely too much on the prior knowledge of a few words.

Although children soon learn to take in words as a whole, they need to understand how words are put together. The distinction between 'aeroplane' and 'hand' is obvious, so that children can tell one from the other because of the shape. But the distinction between 'hard' and 'hand' needs more refined discrimination. Children need to interpret single letters at the same time as recognizing whole words.

Key words

The concept of teaching a few key words is a tempting one, since it is inevitable that children will latch on to what is easily recognized. But such associations are not enough in themselves. Certain longer words, like 'television', children find easy to recognize. Their very length gives an initial clue in distinguishing them from short words such as 'a' and 'the', and their use can facilitate teaching concepts such as the relationship between the length of the written word and the length of its sound, and the idea of labelling. Similarly, it is far easier to recognize the word 'hippopotamus', when it is the only long word in a list, than to distinguish between similar words of roughly the same length, such as 'when', 'where', 'there', 'then' and 'them'.

It is through judicious use of the ability to make visual discriminations that the idea of 'key words' can be recognized from the general indecipherable patterns of reading. The commonest words in print, such as:

a   and   he   I   in   it   of   that   the   to   was

are often as difficult for children to read as any other. This is part of the problem with concentrating on common words as if they were the 'key'.

It is useful for children to be aware which words are most common, but it does not help them to make use of their ability to concentrate merely upon a few words. While children can learn to make almost automatic associations with words, it does not necessarily help them learn to read, in the real sense. Ultimately, of course, children's reading will consist of nothing but key words; the response will be as automatic as a conditioned reflex. But first children need to analyse, for they will surely begin to seek out only those words they already know, and hope for them to appear.

While children are becoming more familiar with the structure of words, we need to remember that they also need to extend their pleasure in the use of words. While the writing system is being explored, the development of vocabulary and the pleasure in stories, together with visual and auditory abilities, all need constant attention. There are moments, especially when children are having frustrating difficulties in reading words, when they may think that recognizing one word means that it will be just as easy to recognize the next, even if it is not familiar. Children may then forget how to go about reading. This happens because they have temporarily forgotten the visual clues, the means of making clear discriminations.

'Diacritical marking'

There is always a gap between the words that children use, and their knowledge of what is written. Sometimes, with fast readers, the mismatch is the other way round; they read with an extensive vocabulary that they do not understand and learn words that they have never heard pronounced. The initial difficulty lies in the fact that the orthographical system is inconsistent: it has certain rules that are simple, others that are complex, and still more that are cheerfully, if occasionally, broken. One way to help children, even at the early stages, is to use a system of marking words, to draw attention to the peculiarity of certain rules. Instead of suggesting that reading is a simple matter and that the fault lies with the child, it is more encouraging to accept the awkward facts of English orthography and show how to tackle them.

'Diacritical' marking is a term for any system used to draw attention to particular difficulties. It is not necessary to invent a huge system of extra linguistic props that almost takes over from the words. It is not necessary to use a system of colour codes that become almost like another way of denoting sounds. A judicious use of occasional marks, like drawing attention to the 'hidden "e"', helps children learn what to look for, without drawing attention away from the graphical signals themselves. A kind of coding can be used to draw out the same sound written in many different ways, as in:

aisle   height   lie   sign   high   island   guide   dye   by

The different pronunciations of a letter like 'a' can be clarified by circling or underlining it. One of the most useful points of clarification can be to draw attention to vowel combinations, so that children know which letters blend into a whole:

night   goat   car   great   green

'Silent' letters can be masked out:

write   right

In one system, a whole range of different markings is used, denoting the exceptions to rules, or noting when the letter 'r' is temporarily raised to a vowel. The problem with too comprehensive a system is that the attempt to reduce the complexities to a manageable set of rules does not fit into the more subtle ways in which children learn to interpret script. Their deciphering of the code needs to take in the variety of different rules, the constantly changing patterns of words. Diacritical marking can help point out how to overcome a particular difficulty at one time, until it has been understood and absorbed.

Word building

Nothing makes children more aware of the constituent parts of words than their own ability to make new words out of given ones. They can be asked to add letters to make new words from, for example, words like 'ear', 'eel' and 'eat', or change the first letter of a word to a different one, in words like 'cat', 'dear', 'cake', 'melt' and 'mat'. They can also build new words out of two words that are given them, taking the relevant syllables to join together, as for example in:

fly   thing   crow   thumb

fling   crumb

One effective way of helping children develop their sense of the ways in which words are written is to ask them to make sense out of a series of jumbled letters. The more children become aware of things turned upside down, or obviously 'wrong', the more aware they become of the basic rules, the 'correct' in contrast. It is sometimes suggested that children always remember something 'wrong', but this assumes that children are like putty upon which every new instruction remains embedded. Children's constant experiment with the world around them depends on their learning the difference between the true and the false, and the more opportunities they have to discover it, the better.

They can make a new word out of jumbled letter cards, possibly with a picture clue. They can point out if a single sentence is true or false, for example, 'coal is green'. They can look at a picture that has three simple descriptions, only one of which is sensible. They can rewrite sentences that do not make sense, or rearrange jumbled words they know into a sentence. They can make up words from given letters or find words within words. They can discriminate between the right and wrong spelling, in sentences such as:

Thing/think before you speak.
The light is bite/bright.

There are many ways, at a variety of levels, in which children enjoy giving order to the material before them. It is then that they acquire that sense of what is correct in the way we write.

Through an awareness of syllables, of affixes and compound words, fluent reading for meaning is developed. This is less complicated than it sounds. It follows on naturally from the abilities to blend and to understand the morphological base on which words are made. It is possible to create quite easy games that give a clear indication of how long words are put together. One of the simplest is to have a 'domino' system for words of two syllables, so that the game is played not by matching but by making up a word, using, for instance:

pet   for   get   jum   per   car

Children can also be asked to put together different words that start or end in the same way. Even if each word is unique, the parts that make up words are flexible and interchangeable. Any game with words, which draws attention to their constituent parts, encourages the ability to identify significant clues to recognition.

The importance of drawing attention to the parts of a word lies in the fact that it is a way of combining the skill of reading with an understanding of meaning. Children are being helped to understand morphemes, those parts of words that make up what it means. A word like 'mis-chance' can be understood if one understands the meaning of its two parts. When children have learnt how to make up new words from combinations such as:

b	at
t	in
d	ot
c	at

they can go on to put new compound words together. One of the simplest ways of drawing attention to parts of the word is by concentrating on a commonly used ending such as 'ing'. When children know words like 'jumping' and 'singing', they sometimes remain half-aware of the meaning of the suffix 'ing'.

Even before children recognize different syllables in their written form, they can be asked to divide spoken words into syllables. They then learn not only how phonemes blend, but how a word is built up. Over 80 per cent of all prefixed words use one of 15 core prefixes (which include, for example, 're', 'ad', 'un', 'in', 'dis', 'de' and 'pro'), and it is worth concentrating on some of these at length.

Children can also be asked to think of different endings for the same word. With a word like 'play' they can think of adding 'ing' or 'ed' or 'er' or 's', and then use these forms in a sentence either written or spoken. With a word like 'fat' you can ask them to think of endings such as 'est' and 'er'. We can teach affixes as units of both sound and meaning, and one realization can help the other. If we teach that words are built up of constituent parts such as:

ab – normal
pre – pare
re – peat

we are helping children not only to recognize letter combinations and important clues but also to realize the significance of them.

We can also teach some distinct grapheme combinations, including 'tion' and 'able', by drawing attention to their significant meanings. Once children are able to recognize simple words easily, and more significantly read simple words they have not come across before, including nonsense words, then it is not a difficult matter to extend their ability to read longer words. One way is to take compound words that are made up of distinct syllabic units such as:

play   ground
ice   cream
milk   shake

and encourage the children to think of others. While doing this, children recognize how a long word can be broken down into distinct parts: they learn, in fact, a technique for the analysis of more complex reading.

They can be asked to divide a polysyllabic word into smaller units. They can be given clues out of which a new word can be derived as in 'pet' and 'car'. They can be given cards on each of which is either the first or second half of a word which they then build. They can be asked to make word patterns from letter blocks such as:

never
ever
even.

Word building draws attention to the connection between reading skills and meaning. Just as the ability to blend was the most important ability in the recognition of syllables, so the recognition of syllables underlies the ability to read more complex words.

There are many games that can be played to encourage the recognition of familiar words. One of the most popular is a version of 'bingo' in which each card carries 12 words, which might either have specific phonic variations, or be obviously different from each other. The teacher can introduce this to small or large groups, and in compèring the game, rely either on the visual recognition of a word, or on the ability to recognize a word that is called out. A variation of dominoes can also be played, with either simple or more complex words being used, such as:

hat	bat		bat	catch

One useful way of developing the recognition of words is to play a type of 'rummy' in which a winning run is a short phrase of three words that makes sense, such as:

A		cold		night

so that children not only recognize the words but put them into a meaningful context. At a simpler level of recognition the children can play 'happy families', with either the same words, or words of the same 'family'. Such a game can be as simple as matching pictures, or more complex, demanding some knowledge of particular concepts, such as words to do with animals, as opposed to those to do with furniture.

Any task in which words are matched to each other familiarizes children with the specific words to be remembered and with the particular clues that distinguish one word from another. It is usually more effective to encourage a pair of children to work together than to create large team games with competitions, since the kind of help children can give each other can be very useful.

In all tasks involving either matching words or recognizing them, it is helpful to give words meaning by using them in sentences. It is not enough to make children respond automatically to a word in isolation, without knowing what it means. One of the simplest ways of combining the recognition of words with their meaning is to teach pairs that go together, supported by pictures: 'bat and ball', 'dustpan and brush', 'fish and chips'. Later on, children can learn to write out these words on a visual clue, or put the right labels on the right picture.

The recognition of whole words is not an automatic process. It is not helpful for children to repeat the same sounds unless they are aware of their meaning. The ability to recognize certain words teaches children to take in clues more sophisticated than a letter. We are not teaching them to memorize 'whole' words, but teaching them to spot the important clues in a more sophisticated and less painstaking manner. The importance of 'key' words lies in the fact that they are clues to the developing ability to read.

One of the ways of encouraging children's ability to recognize whole words is to ask them to use blocks with letters on them, and change the order of the blocks around to see how many words they can make up. The recognition of whole words is just a larger version of the recognition of individual letters; it develops the ability to understand more clues at once, from analysing the direction and shape of every letter, to recognizing a whole series of letters.

We can develop children's familiarity with words by making use of their sense of context, and their sense of the meaning of words. We can present a sentence in which they can choose one of three possible words, once they have been told what the rest of the sentence means, for example:

$$
\begin{array}{ccc}
 & \text{doll} & \\
\text{I like to} & \text{hit} & \text{to the circus} \\
 & \text{go} &
\end{array}
$$

We can also do the same thing while giving a clue to the word they will complete, as in:

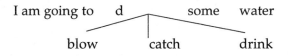

To encourage close attention to all parts of words it is helpful to ask children to pick out nonsense words from sets of otherwise correct ones, especially if you are at the same time concentrating on particular digraphs. Examples are:

rock	pock	rake
bake	sock	pake

One development of this process of understanding words is to make children think of other conceptual meanings that connect the words. Children can be asked to put together words that by their sense belong together, such as:

nose	eat
ears	smell
mouth	hear

As a way of substantiating a familiarity with words, children can be asked to connect a simple picture with the word that describes it, for example:

here is a 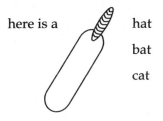 hat

bat

cat

Other simple games that bolster their ability to recognize and predict include 'word relay', in which two teams take it in turns to recognize words and use them in sentences, and 'word snap'. Children can also be asked to cite as many words as they know from what they see in the streets, or from signs or shop fronts.

The development of children's knowledge of simple words can also be helped by use of the game 'jotto'. This is played between two people, both of whom think of a word of four letters, each of which must be different. Each player takes it in turn to guess a letter, and the other player tells them if this letter is included in their word. They are not told where the letter is placed in the word. By clever guesses and by predicting spellings, this game can be played to a fair degree of sophistication while not demanding an extensive vocabulary.

Chapter 13
Reading for meaning

The awareness of the particular skill of reading can sometimes become a hindrance in the development of what reading is for: the communication and learning of ideas. Children can become entangled in the difficulty of spelling out words when they are also looking for the chance to recognize them instantly. They face the problem that the techniques fluent readers use are not merely speeded-up versions of the approaches early readers make. The breakthrough from one reading technique to another, from the consciousness of individual letters, or even individual words, to the recognition of those significant clues which translate the code into meaning, is sometimes rapid but sometimes very awkward.

Fluent readers can scan more script than they can read aloud. They both guess and assume what is in the text, and they tend to use the written signals as a kind of confirmation of what they expect. As well as taking in several words in one fixation of the eye, fluent readers need only a minimum number of marks to recognize what they see. The upper half of a line of print can be read much more easily than the bottom half, since the more significant differences are held there.

If this sentence is written out and divided into two the fact can be demonstrated

If this sentence is written out and divided into two the fact can be demonstrated

Fluent readers have learnt to do without many of the details that they first had to learn. The first level of reading is as slow as reading this:

dnuor yaw thgir eht siht gnidaer yrt

Readers are so accustomed to certain phrases that even the way in which a sentence is formed on a page makes a difference to the ease with which it is read. The first pattern of words that follows is more difficult to read than the second:

During World War
II even fantastic
schemes received
consideration if they gave
promise of shortening the
conflict.

During World War II
even fantastic schemes
received consideration
if they gave promise
of shortening the conflict.

Expert typesetters are aware of the importance of layout and the choice of breaks; such awareness is not always apparent in books for children.

For a fluent reader, it is as easy to identify a word as to identify a single letter standing in isolation. We can help children make the shift from the moment when every feature is significant – for example, 'b' and 'da' – to when there are certain features that are recognized, by trying to make as much sense as possible out of the task of reading. When children are familiar with the uses of language they can respond to the sentences, understanding the inevitability and the consistency of print. Even the syntactic structure of sentences makes a difference to the ease of reading. For example, the first line of this nonsense verse is easier to read than the second:

The toves wur slithing hum a mome rath.
Rath hum toves a slithing mome the wur.

When a sentence fits an expected pattern, the significant clues are far easier to recognize. Cloze technique shows that we can guess the meanings of a sentence even when there are words left out. We do not even need every letter:

Si–e -t -s po–i-l- t- m-k- se-n– -f t-i-.

Fluent readers are not only able to guess the missing letters in a word, or the missing words in a sentence, but can make 'bridging assumptions' about the texts they read. They look for clues that fit in to what they expect, so that some texts are far easier to read than others. It is easy to process script if there is no shift in the topic; more difficult to incorporate different information. The reader always takes in two or three words in one eye movement, and children need to learn how to take in more than one word at the same time. Too many eye movements retard both fluency and comprehension. Skilled readers make use of the meanings of words ahead of fixation to enrich their interpretation of the text, or use those words more simply as markers to guide future eye movements to the location of the next useful fixation.

However fast we read, we do not respond just to words. Although words are the most significant units of meaning, we do not read by undertaking an excursion from word to word. For one thing, every reader scans both words and sentences not just in one constant flow but in a series of saccadic movements. The eyes jump from point to point, but respond to particular resting places within each line. Although we recognize every word, almost instantaneously, however long, we do so not by running our eyes along it, but by travelling over it backwards as well as forwards. For an adult reader this is a sub-conscious process; for the early reader it is a necessary one, since words are only units of distinct meaning when the last letter, which like the 'hidden "e"' might change all, is seen. Fluent readers make 'sense' of what they see by interpreting it, by knowing which clues are significant and which can be passed over. Reading is the recognition of significant meanings.

We cannot confront children with whole words and expect them to know how to read, for they learn by their ability to blend. But there comes a time when the recognition of words seems automatic, when the need is to learn to recognize a word without conscious analysis, even if analysis is what actually takes place. We can help by developing children's ability to know easy words, so that they can concentrate on analysing the more difficult ones. Whole words depend, like road signs, on clues and on context. They are also a direct link to the larger, more linguistic, process of thinking without the barrier of interpretation.

Reading can never be dissociated from meaning. The child who stumbles through a reading scheme without understanding has to relearn how to read properly. There is an anecdote about a boy who, having just read a passage fluently to the class and asked to explain it, said, 'I don't know; I wasn't listening.' Those difficult moments in children's lives when they cannot make sense of the letters and they lose the desire to concentrate often come about because the process seems so meaningless. It is then that the guessing becomes an escape, a desire for an easy way out of the problem, rather than an essential means of predicting what will come next.

> Once I was trying to read a word and I couldn't find out what this word was and I went to Miss . . ., it was 'the' and because I couldn't read it I was ever so frightened because she kept going on and on and on . . .
>
> (boy, 10)

The teacher's, or parent's, own example of reading is of the utmost importance. The sharing of stories should never be thought of as appropriate only for the youngest children, since stories are not only important in their own right but constantly remind children about the purpose of reading. The very facts that writing communicates and can easily be understood, and that it is a form of sharing, support children's sense of the relationship between meaning and writing. The more closely children learn to follow and attend to a story, the more closely they will learn to look for the relevant clues in a text. It can be helpful and stimulating to read most of a story that children finish for themselves. They can be asked to predict what will happen from the clues they have already been given.

Another way of encouraging children to listen carefully to language is to ask them to describe a piece of drama to each other. If a few children are asked to act a scene, another group of children can be asked to describe exactly what happened, to a third group who did not see it. This third group can then be asked to enact the same drama from the instructions they have been given, and the two versions compared. Children can also be asked to make up a story together: one child begins it, and the others continue it in turn. Children can also be asked to describe just one moment in the middle of a story. They can then discuss what they think would happen next. They can also compare what they think is going to happen in the middle of a story to what actually happens in the written text. The degrees of difference can be very varied.

One simple means of helping children see the use of reading is to make use of written instructions as well as verbal ones. Children will, to some extent, guess what the instructions are, and become familiar with both the context and the recognizable repeated statements. Children can be asked to draw pictures according to a series of very simple instructions. From these clues they can tell whether they should draw a man or a house. Children can also try to pick out a sentence that describes a particular picture, finding a clue such as a word they recognize and discovering to which picture the sentence refers.

There was a time when any suggestion that children should interpret particular clues or make guesses was severely discouraged. There is, however, an important distinction between guessing as a way of withdrawing from even looking at words, and guessing as a way of predicting through knowledge of the context. Some mistakes that children make can be seen as 'miscues', a matter of making the wrong prediction based on a sensible understanding of the context. Since reading is so much a matter of using all kinds of clues, this is not a bad thing. Children can be encouraged to correct themselves.

Children's tendency to make consistent approximations can get in the way of their making the specifically correct judgement about a particular letter. Children can be encouraged to help each other, by reading to each other from an early stage, and by picking out exact clues and sharing their understanding. They can then motivate each other to discover the exact correspondence between the written and the spoken.

Certain words are distinctive and readily recognized – 'television' is a typical example – and can be given early and used often so that children become accustomed to seeing words whole. But children need the ability, not only to recognize instantly, but to analyse. It is useful, once they are familiar with such words, to continue to remind them how the words are made up, even if the words are difficult. It is for this reason that children should be encouraged to learn to recognize their own names, and also, as far as possible, the names of others.

Fluency is itself so important that children should also read things that are very easy for them. Just as children do not need to be discouraged from reading beyond their own 'age', so it is useful practice to let children read simpler material fairly fast. The strategies a child uses in reading are too complex to be thought of in terms of set 'stages'. There have been occasions when children have entered school as fairly fluent readers only to be told to go through the same primitive reading scheme that all the other children are following. The parent's answer to the teacher's hint that reading should be left to the school is to wonder whether using language should also be left to the school.

The use of stories

The connection between children's increasing experience and their understanding of it lies in the uses of familiarity. Children find it easier to recognize the familiar than to recall it. A word used more than once becomes part of a child's contextual vocabulary; and a word seen several times becomes familiar even before it carries a particular meaning. Children will cling to what is familiar; they will want to know better what they already know. The desire to hear the same pattern of a story, to have each word in its own place, to exchange the same remarks: all these are part of a child's developing mastery.

The desire for the familiar can not only be explained; it can also be used. Children like to hear the same story again and again as if it were a good piece of music or a poem, just as they like to read the same story again and again. This is true not only of those older children who have a favourite book, but of those children who are still learning to read. It is a fact which can be exploited if children like the material. Holding up a few flash cards at the start of every day is not the version of familiarity recommended here. It does not further children's natural love of language. One of the most successful methods of teaching reading to those who have some of the basic skills is through children's familiarity with particular stories.

The idea is to help children learn to read a complete story of their own choice, and to do so by encouraging them to repeat reading it until they know it by heart. Each child should choose a story of his or her own, because each one's own motivation is important. It does not matter if the story is beyond the child's ostensible 'level' or if it has been chosen for its pictures. The teacher first reads the story through with the child. The child follows the text, knowing that the next step is to learn to read it without the teacher. The most useful device in this process is the tape recorder. Once the teacher has recorded the story, the child can follow it again and again until he or she is utterly familiar with it. Once children are completely familiar with a text, they will not only have learnt to recognize important clues, but will understand what it feels like to read a story through. Once children have mastered one story, they will find another one rather easier.

There is a sense of security in going over the same material again; it answers the same need that children feel when, at an early stage, they are forever building up and knocking down the same pile of bricks. With the tape recorder children can also listen to themselves reading. This can be done in one of two ways: by comparing themselves to the master tape, or by following their own reading to make certain of its accuracy. The art of learning a particular story can be extended by allowing children, once they have mastered a story and made it their own, to read it to each other. This is also a boost to their confidence.

Any familiarity with what children like can be used to promote their confidence in their own memory. The more they are asked to recognize the same material, the more they will feel that they have something substantial to depend on, just as children like to go over well-trodden ground in a subject such as maths. The desire to test knowledge is a fundamental one in children; from the earliest age they make a ritual of exploring their own familiar abilities. This repetitive exercise can seem to adults to be rather mechanical and uncreative, but it is a necessary part of children's ability to learn. The security of the familiar is as important as those sudden leaps of understanding, since learning is not just a matter of a steady accumulation of knowledge.

The most important principle underlying children's familiarity with material is that whatever they become accustomed to should mean something and be enjoyable. Many children will not give their attention to single words. Familiar words in the context of a story are quite another thing. One of the most useful techniques in dealing with a complete story with a whole group of children is to make up a wall display. The complete story, together with their illustrations to it, can be put up on the walls and retold by the teacher and by individual children. This is rather like putting up a book where all can read it, and it is of far greater interest to children than individual labels on furniture.

There are many ways in which displays on the walls can actively be used. Children can learn a story through a sequence of pictures interpreted in a number of ways. They then discuss what words would be used to explain the illustrations, which helps them understand the use of script, and also teaches them sequencing, logic and interpretation. Children can also discuss in which order to put a series of pictures so that some kind of story emerges.

We need to combine the familiar with the more sophisticated, especially as memory (for shapes and sounds as well as words) consists of the ability to store complexities through familiarity. It is useful to give children tasks that extend their memory, like drawing a picture they have seen before or a shape that they should be familiar with, until it is 'printed' on their minds. Later, children will be able to remember whole sequences of words.

One variation of this technique of extending children's confidence through familiarity is to use simple comic strips, blanking out the bubbles in which speech is printed. Children can be asked to put the pictures into sequence, and to explain the story. They can also be asked to say what they think each character is saying. At this stage the words can be written in. Children will then have thought about the script in the strip rather than, as usually happens, ignoring it for the sake of the pictures. They will also begin to understand written dialogue.

Young children will wish to learn a story they like, but they will also want things written down for them. It is worth taking any opportunity to write out for a child whatever he or she wants to say; whether it is a statement or a caption. Children have something to express, and seeing it expressed helps them understand the whole reading process. With older children who are slow readers, one of the most successful techniques is the simple one of helping them to learn to read from whatever arises naturally out of their own enthusiasm or interest. When they see the point of reading, their confidence in the task and in their memory is greatly enhanced.

The use of writing

Some of the most simple and effective ways of teaching reading are based on the need to involve children in expressing what they want to say. The technique of writing down those statements a learner wishes to make about a particular interest of his or her own is one example. Memorizing a favourite story until it can be repeated exactly is another.

A significant reason for an early encouragement of writing is that it encourages the understanding of the shape of letters; it is a kinaesthetic way of teaching reading. It also demonstrates the uses of reading. For this reason a teacher should take every opportunity to be seen writing, to illustrate its use, and to be interested in what children write. The more that written work is seen as a means of communication, the better. Even when children are unable to write fluently, they can be encouraged to try to write things down, even if it emerges as a kind of parody of 'real' writing. Children like to think that they are able to write. They assume at first that the series of marks on a page will mean something, not because they make the naïve assumption that the teacher will understand, but because they are demonstrating the action of writing, and thereby showing that they have grasped its essential purpose.

The words that children have thought of for themselves will be far easier for them to read than those that are unfamiliar. Even the most used word, like the child's own name, however comparatively complex, can be a means for that child to come to an understanding of the form of letters and their symbolic purpose. Just tracing one or two words is not enough; children needs to be encouraged to write on their own so that the formation of script ends up with some meaning. Even in simple sentences it is worth making the child respond to the need to write. Cloze procedure, deleting a few words in a paragraph and asking children to fill them in, can also be useful. Children can be asked to write in the words that they think are missing, and learn by contextual clues what words would make sense: a combination of intelligent response and a particular task. A simple variation on this is to give the clue to the word by an initial letter, or else by providing an indication of the shape of the word:

'Once upon a t . . . there was a little ⌐⌐ who . . .'

Even at the earliest stages of reading children can be encouraged to think about what they are doing. Their capacity to learn and use their minds is underrated, partly because we assume that their reading is confined to a laborious building-up of simple clues until at last they can make use of them in an intelligent way. Only when their knowledge, their response, and their perceptions are all applied to the task are they using their real capacity. Even when they are starting to read, we can ask them to create a sentence out of the simple words that they have learnt.

Reading is often more difficult when it is very slow, for it is too easy to lose the sense of the meaning. One reason for the usefulness of children's writing is that it provides a means of helping them sustain themselves through the labour of learning the parts that make up a word. There is often a gap between what children want to say and their ability to write it. Their learning to write is a form of disciplining themselves to their own appropriate pace. Once children have written even one line of print, they have overcome some of the problems of reading; they will have comprehended not only simple matters like left to right orientation, but the more complex concept of joining letters into words, which results in a statement. Writing is itself a means of clarifying technical points such as lower and upper case.

Writing can be used in a variety of ways, from initial simple recording of what children want to have written, to their capacity to express something original. Handwriting exercises should never be divorced from the use of writing; the sheer mechanics of script never make any sense in themselves. Instead of any mechanical copying children can write to some purpose, whether this be in the form of putting together magazines, anthologies or writing letters. Stories that the children have made up or remember can be shared through writing them out. They can also be illustrated by other children once they are written out. Comic strips can be a means of helping children to write some simple messages; or children can be asked to illustrate a few sentences in comic-strip form. They can also make pin-men illustrations for a series of sentences, or draw in these pin-men around 'speech-bubbles' that have been drawn for them. The written material can be simple, but the level of sophistication in interpreting the situation is far more advanced.

When writing is used for a clear purpose it is less likely to be seen as boring. When children's minds are being challenged, there is a far greater chance that they will apply themselves to those clues that make sense. An example of this is to ask children to write a simple caption to a picture. They will not be expected to say the obvious – the picture could be quite hard to interpret – but their task of writing will oblige them to concentrate both on the words they use in speech and on those they know how to write, while also seeing the difference. They can later be asked to write a caption for a newspaper picture. They can also be asked to write a simple description of a picture, again adapting their ability in writing to their ability to interpret the picture. Having reached the level of being able to write a fairly coherent analysis of a picture, other children can be asked to interpret their description by drawing their own version of the picture.

There will be times, however, when children wish to practise their writing even if it has no ostensible purpose. When children wish to copy, let them choose their own material; when copying is initiated by the children themselves, it should be encouraged. This mechanical repetition of a story is, in fact, a labour both of love and of the child's need.

Part four

Developing reading skills

'What's the use of their having names,' the Gnat said, 'if they won't answer to them?'

'No use to *them*,' said Alice, 'but it's useful to the people that name them, I suppose. If not, why do things have names at all?'

(Lewis Carroll, *Through the Looking Glass*, Chapter 3)

Chapter 14
Fluent reading

The fluent reader forgets about the process of reading, and concentrates on the rewards of reading. Even in difficult passages the awareness of difficulty resides in what the text means, or tries to mean, rather than in the negotiations with graphemes. But many children, caught in that gap between the learning of the specific skill, and the use made of that skill, have the uneasy tendency to revert to the consciousness of the act of reading, like a person suddenly self-conscious about driving a car. It is this subconscious memory of the difficulties of the task that can make some people unwilling to read anything but the least demanding material, and that can make some people suffer from 'word blindness'. A truly fluent reader has become so accustomed to the uses of reading, that, like driving a car, they take it for granted. The fluent reader remains in constant practice.

Reading becomes a skill we take for granted when it becomes a pleasure for its own sake, as well as a central means by which facts and ideas are conveyed and learnt. To explore a text for the information to be copied out as part of a topic is not the true end of reading. The ability to look for relevant information derives from the delight in reading for sustained periods, with the assumption that more subtle matters, emotional and imaginative as well as factual, are being internalized. Those children who have become accustomed to the pleasures of reading are generally more articulate and find study more gratifying. If the earliest stages of reading convey some of that imaginative pleasure – the love of stories and the excitement of finding out about words – then the skill will more easily be translated into use.

One of the most constructive ways of encouraging the use of reading and the extension of fluency is to help children convey information that interests them. This is a subtle skill, since it requires an awareness of the individual interests of children, and a knowledge of what techniques are appropriate in the development of their writing. At the simplest level, children should be asked to write about what interests them, not just the news of events over the weekend, but ideas and emotions. Such writing is closely allied to discussion and to reading, for it all depends on children having a purpose that appeals to them, rather than a troubled curiosity devoted to guessing what the teacher seems to be demanding. Children's writing can demand a high level of thought, so that they have to find the right words with which to convey their ideas, rather than adapting their thoughts to the limitations of their vocabulary.

This attempt to find out and encourage pupils to write about what interests them, so that they discover the pleasures of finding the right words to convey their ideas and feelings, is even more significant if we contrast it to many of the tasks that are given to children. Too often they are given a tired subject, which they do not wish to pursue: 'my weekend' or 'my holiday'. The association of school with certain kinds of demand tends to cut off a whole range of interests that remain separate and private. Having an essay title imposed can only be interesting if it is also seen as a challenge, like the challenge of talking to a theme for a minute in the radio programme. Many of the tasks presented to children in school are quite unlike what happens in the world outside. Think how often pupils have been asked to write a story or a novel, on one side or two sides of A4, or in a limited amount of time. This is both an unnatural and a difficult task. The art of the short story is complex, but those we actually read as adults are quite unlike what is set in schools. There are many alternative means of extending writing skills, most of which are based on the premise that any task demanded of pupils should be recognizably like one they would experience in their normal lives outside school. Parody is often a great help.

There are many ways in which the abilities to use language, and convey ideas in writing, can be extended. A game like 'twenty quest-ions', with its use of categories, which teaches children to ask certain types of question, to make predictions and to understand the varieties of discrimination, can be played in verbal or written form. The ability of children to extend their useful vocabulary can be helped by encour-aging them to find alternatives for particular words in a sentence. They can be asked to write a sentence that includes a given list of words – for example, 'A book, Dr Johnson, red, case, sun' – a task which probes their imaginative use of words, and tests their the ability to see the extent of the possible syntax that could be used. As children begin to learn the different kinds of reading, they can be helped by exploring dimensions both of abstraction – the conveying of information – and of the personal, by the use of diaries, letters, short 'autobiographies' and narratives. And while they are thinking of the uses to which language can be put, they can also, with the aid of dictionaries, look for the meanings of words. Teachers can use a device as simple as asking pupils to think of a word of one letter beginning with 'a', a word of two letters beginning with 'b', three letters beginning with 'c', four with 'd', and so on, and make as coherent a sentence out of the results as they can. Children can also be asked to think of as many sentences as they can which could be interpreted ambiguously, according to the way in which they are *spoken*, rather than written. Examples are:

> When he entered the room, Mary kissed John.
> He left me to get on with the job.

Once children have acquired the essential facility of decoding words, their improvement depends on the amount of time they spend using this ability. They deserve to be given as much time as possible for extended reflective reading. The reading that children need consists of more than copying out tracts from set sources. The use of textbooks on topics can sometimes seem to children little more than copying out, rather than thinking about, information; it is then only at home that reading becomes a significant part of learning. The problem is that our system of testing, upon which so much of the curriculum can depend, tends to demand little more than a repetition of known facts; it rarely demands more thought or a personal point of view. It is, after all, very easy to set comprehension tests that demand no understanding whatsoever of the text being tested. A rudimentary knowledge of syntax is enough in most cases. Many tests could be translated into nonsense, and still as easily answered. For example:

> The mugly glat vimbled squidgely in the stanchy flong.
>
> q. What kind of glat was it?
> q. What was it doing?
> q. Where was it doing this?
> q. How was it doing it?   etc.

Traditional comprehension tests, based on short passages, are not the most satisfactory way of improving the ability to read with understanding.

Reading only becomes the automatic ability we take for granted when it is used for something we do not take for granted, something new and interesting. When we read in such a way the words are hurried over, we anticipate what will happen next, and are so tuned to the familiar that we fail to spot the redundant words like 'the' when there are too many of them, as we fail to spot the many mistakes traditionally linked with the Grauniad newspaper. We can fluently read nonsense that is syntactically sound:

When we came to go out is to laugh wildly and squash the cat.

but stumble on nonsense that is syntactically aberrant:

Probity fishing only circumspect going full.

Children learn how to read in different styles, according to the circumstances in which they find themselves. Their balance of close attention to the text, and awareness of what the text conveys, can be helped by 'playing' with language, by turning many ideas upside-down. The more children are aware of what does *not* fit, the more they become aware of those rules that are consistent. Just as there are many ways of jumbling letters, of re-patterning sentences, so there are ways of extending children's idea of the 'norms' of language by, for example, knowing familiar verbal pairings:

Bread and
Fish and
Knife and

Much of the material that children use comes from the familiar and the everyday. They need to learn to pay attention even to those things that they most often ignore, like television. The tendency to separate the 'work' of school from the 'play' of home is actually based on the assumption that after an exhausting day's work it is possible to close the mind down, to put it at a different level of functioning. While children can use different styles of reading, and different levels of attention, according to the task in hand, the danger is that children find one kind of inattention so easy that they find it hard to apply themselves to many of the activities they carry out. In reading, attention is an emotional attitude; a willingness to apply the mind to the problem in hand, and a skill, the ability to see what the task consists of.

Attention

Some of the problems of reading come about when children find it difficult to pay close attention. This is true of both their listening and their looking. Some children know the names of many stars from television or radio, but their spelling of the names reveals not only that they have not seen them written out, but that even the most familiar names are heard only in the most general way. Another example of their difficulties is the reversal or substitution of letters. This derives from the fact that they are not looking closely. What children need is not so much a regurgitation of what they have already learnt, but training in more complex perception, to accustom them to look at things precisely. It is interesting to note how many miscues come because a child jumps on to some kind of meaning, without having the ability to take in a larger amount of information at the same time. Thus, when

Jan was a lovely girl

turns into

Jan saw a lovely girl

it shows that the reader has not thought of the possibility that the rest of the sentence could reveal something different, and has not been careful enough with particular words.

One way of encouraging close attention is to make use of written instructions like 'Draw a house', or 'Put three windows in', so that the children make sure of accuracy and carry out the exact instructions. They can then be asked to describe what they have drawn so that the accuracy is carried over into their written work. It is common for children not to look closely at what they have themselves written; the mistakes often derive from a lack of care rather than ignorance.

Another way of helping children look for accuracy in both writing and drawing is to have a series of pictures, rather like 'Identikits', made up from different features. They can be asked to put together the Identikit picture that fits a particular description; or they can be asked to find the description to fit a picture. Close observation, allied to memory, can also be fostered by showing children some pictures and asking questions about them later, when the pictures have been put away. This can be done with portraits or with pictures which are full of details.

The ability to see accurately can be encouraged by questions based either on pictures or on television shows children have seen, or been asked to see. But the ability to listen also needs encouragement. One can accept the differences between speech and print, but it does make life difficult for children if they have not been taught to listen accurately. 'Perfick' is Dickens's example, but there are many mispronunciations such as 'skelington' which compound the difficulties. A 'feel' for the sound of words can be encouraged by a variation of Bartlett's ideas of 'Mallomas' and 'Taketis'. Here he suggested that a word like 'balloon' would sound soft and flexible, and a word like 'icicle' harsh and edgy. Hence one was a 'malloma' and the other a 'taketi' or, symbolized in drawings:

Children have an instinctive sense of the 'feel' of words. They can put a list of words under each heading, or more interestingly can invent their own names for these categories as well as define them. One of the most useful ways of extending children's consciousness of words and sounds is to ask them to pay close attention to songs; to unscramble what a song is saying. It is also noticeable that while many children can 'sing along' with a song, can mouth what is happening when they recognize it, they find it almost impossible to recall the words without a cue, for that demands a very much more precise level of attention.

Close attention and interpretation are matters of semantic clues as well as visual and auditory ones. Many headlines in newspapers lend themselves to analysis, because they show many of the problems that we take for granted, but which can cause difficulties to those who are unaccustomed to them. Take for example a typical headline:

BBC		STRIKE
OFF		AFTER
2½	pc	OFFER

This is very simple once we have understood the basic layout, and the context to which it refers. Who made the offer? How do we know it was concerned with pay? 2½ per cent of what? But we also have to learn what symbols stand for, despite the lack of punctuation, and what letters like 'pc' mean.

Headlines, like photographs and television pictures, are a kind of code, and they draw attention to the kind of skills involved in interpretation. They also create a problem in being written for people who do not automatically pay attention, who are not actually seeking out information. Children continue to need to look at those things they could habitually ignore. It is worth comparing a book, which is being read, to one which is being shown on television. We can draw attention to the details by asking children to look for particular clues in a film. They can also be made to look attentively at comics by being asked to rearrange a series of pictures into a possible sequence, and see how many alternatives there are. All these techniques teach more about reading than they seem to do at first glance, for they encourage the ability to concentrate with perception.

Enlarging the reading vocabulary

Nothing is more important in any learning than the acquisition of a large and well-used vocabulary. The complexities of grammar, and the complexities of thought, are dependent on the availability of individual words that define, in relation to each other, exactly what the writer wishes to say. The development of a wide vocabulary and the ability to make out the meaning and probable sound of new words are features of another stage in reading. Such extension depends on curiosity, on a desire to know what words can do, what they can express or mean, or imply.

New words are learnt through use; not through the learning of lists, nor through the recitation of synonyms or definitions. For fluent reading, even before we are warned about style, we need to pick up the ability to recognize and make sense of words that look, at first glance, complex and erudite. The ability to read difficult words can be aided as successfully by attention to the unusual as by an analysis of the highly specialized. Children's awareness of the structure of words can be encouraged when they invent new words, or use such words in peculiar contexts in which their meaning is self-evident.

Advertisements often use words in an esoteric way, inventing names of products, or using a particular kind of language. The very act of discovering words which are unusual and which can be defined, and understood by the way in which they are used, is a development of the ability to read. Newspapers are themselves an abundant source of new words, both because of the curiously specialized language dictated by limitations of space ('quit, probe, boost, blitz') and by the way this same vocabulary is used, sometimes in the most peculiar way. Many of the words used in headlines are employed very differently from their original meaning: asking students to analyse the connection between this usage and the conventional usage will interest them far more than trying to teach definitions of words in the style of a test.

Curiosity about words is a natural state in young children, for whom it is a basic necessity without which learning could not take place. This automatic interest is not sustained, unless it is deliberately fostered. The need for the right word derives from the sense that there is only one word that conveys exactly what we mean. It is possible to make oneself understood even with a limited vocabulary. There are many general words that will carry with them enough meaning to substitute for what could be said, but in the end this becomes a limitation. There is nothing so powerful as the example of other people using new words as naturally as leaves come to a tree. Young children experience this every day. From the time all words are new to them, when they build up their vocabulary bit by bit and when they are constantly confronted with new words, they demonstrate their eclectic ability to learn through use, experience and context.

For some, this period of linguistic exploration comes to an end, and literacy in the full sense remains diminished. There are a number of reasons for this. There is an assumption that popularity and appeal lies in the 'average', defined as the undemanding. There is an association of rich vocabulary with jargon, with an impenetrable academic language that is designed to discourage any approaches. Above all, the curriculum as presented through the assessment system as stressing the necessity for skills instead of explaining their purpose. Critical thinking has as central a place as emotional exploration.

Children know that teachers should have enthusiasm and curiosity themselves, but assume that an interest in words is the province of the linguist or specialist in literature. The sad fact is that children's earliest interests in language can be diminished by their experience, when textbooks demand anything but curiosity, and teachers as well as pupils revert to the limited range of verbal gestures that covers having little to say. Children's interest in complex vocabulary is not just a late, technical accomplishment. From the beginning of the teaching of reading there are some words that by their use and relevance are interesting to children. All texts presented to them can be designed to contain at least *one* word that is unfamiliar and demands the ability to understand it from its context, which will be relevant to the subject being discussed.

New words should be experienced before being defined, for this is the natural process of learning. Rather than explaining a technical term like 'erosion' only by a dictionary definition, it is preferable to show it being used in a sentence. Then it is clear *why* the word exists, for there are no such things as exact synonyms. Substituting one adjective for another, or choosing some out of a list, hoping that one will apply, is not a technique that brings many rewards. It is rather more useful to try to apply what seems an appropriate interpretation to a picture, perhaps of a face with a distinctive expression. The need to use a new word should derive from the sense that there is an appropriate description if it could only be found. If children merely fill in blanks with possible or 'correct' solutions chosen from among a limited number of options, they will not have 'read' a new word in any real sense, but merely accustomed themselves to fulfilling a set task. We can use subtle differences between words fairly similar to each other, like clustering different adjectives around two different objects.

Many word games can be used to teach children to look closely at the way in which words are formed. Substituting initial letters (or other letters) to form new words is one simple way of combining close reading with semantics. Anagrams, especially with a pictorial clue to the scrambled letters, is another. One can also ask children to see which two words contained within two different sentences can go together to make a third word. At the simplest, the word 'forget' can be seen to emerge from:

He came for tea.
Why get so upset?

Popular riddles can also be adapted to extend children's interest in different words, to encourage them to think of clues and to apply their growing ability to read. But it has been stressed before that the recognition of whole words depends both on the knowledge of how to go about constructing a word, and on an awareness of, and interest in, its meaning. For this reason children should be encouraged to think of words which will fit with particular morphological suffixes:

er	farmer
ent	parent
tion	correction
able	kickable
less	witless

or prefixes such as:

| pre | prejudge |
| mis | mistake |

On a more sophisticated level pupils should be asked to make new types of words out of the basic semantic root, such as changing 'sign' to 'signature', or 'hard' to 'harden'. They can also see how many words can be created from the basis of a word like 'nation', which can be used to form 'nationalize', 'nationalism' and so on. In this way they will become aware of the roots of words, and less nervous at those words that seem, at first glance, to be incorrigibly long.

It can seem tempting to try to increase children's reading vocabulary by giving them lists of words and asking them to substitute for each another word with a similar meaning. Any glance at *Roget's Thesaurus* will, however, show how dissimilar words are; they might have only slightly different nuances, but they are not exact synonyms, nevertheless. Words are not mere labels for things. Finding the apposite word can be useful, and is more interesting as an exercise in increasing vocabulary.

An awareness of new words and their meaning can also be encouraged by the use of puns. At the very simplest level puns can be 'homographs' – words that have different meanings in different contexts – such as 'I can' and 'In a can'. The stress should be on *using* puns in sentences rather than on recognizing familiar ones.

A series of pictures of people wearing a variety of different clothes can demand not only that pupils describe what they see (this could also be a parody of fashion journalese) but that they give preferences and reasons for their taste. Identikit pictures can be made up from descriptions of different features; the pupil's task is to find the most exact word, rather than the obvious one, to describe the result. Pupils can also be asked to think of all the different ways in which the same word can be used (turn, turn-on, turncoat, turnabout). Cloze procedure can be used at more sophisticated levels, taking as starting points examples from newspapers or journals. The more difficult words do not have to be blanked out; on the contrary, the ability to fill in the blanks should depend on understanding some of the more erudite words in the text.

Every adult reader is bound to come across new words; there is no point at which everything is familiar. Yet we can, superficially at least, know how we ought to pronounce the word; and we know, even by the context, something about its meaning. The word might look familiar and yet be used in a different way, or contain a curiously individual meaning, clear only to the author or a small group, a phenomenon that heralds the beginning of jargon. Nevertheless we have learnt how to absorb the occasional new; children, who come across the new frequently, need to learn the same techniques. When they know the rudiments of reading they still need to know how to learn new words, how to develop their vocabularies and listen with discrimination.

One of the most useful devices in developing language, of course, is the tape recorder, which can be used not only to play passages recorded from the radio, but also to play back to the pupils their own reading of a difficult passage. Children listening to themselves will be slightly embarrassed; but they will also become aware of the importance of inflexion and expression. Reading at this level is closely allied to semantics, to an extensive vocabulary, and to the ability to communicate as well as receive ideas.

Chapter 15
The use of books

Books are what reading is for. Reading has a variety of uses, from understanding signs and tax demands to obtaining information from newspapers, journals, e-mails and the World Wide Web. Books, however, still contain the kind of information and the kinds of human experience that define people's understanding. For young children who have the experience of them, books remain central. The promise of a story, of excitement, of anticipation and the sense of an ending are all symbolized by books. They are definitions of education, of learning as well as pleasure.

Many children discover how to read both by observing and joining in the experience of books and by finding their own means of having access to them. 'Real books' (as they are sometimes called for younger readers) and literature (as it becomes) are central. The use of books, as defined here, is somewhat more specialized, and is invoked for those who do not find the experience natural, or come to it early. Certain texts, closely printed and specialized, present an insuperable barrier. Others, illustrated and simplified, appear more appropriate for beginning readers. Out of this simple distinction has arisen a whole industry of matching texts, through size of print and control of vocabulary, to the perceived needs of the child.

There is a great temptation to rely on reading schemes. The idea behind them is sensible and pragmatic. The carefully organized grading of vocabulary seems logical, the combination of pictures and texts appears attractive, and the fact that all is prepared for the teacher is a relief for those in beleaguered circumstances, short of resources, short of time, short of encouragement and, most of all, short of help. A reading scheme is easy to administer; children seem to make progress from day to day, and it seems a simple matter to assess their progress. Add to this the publisher's interests in marketing such a lucrative package, and one can see why reading schemes are widespread.

Despite their popularity, reading schemes have also been extensively criticized at two different levels. At one level they have been seen to be out of touch with the everyday experience of the majority of their readers; their language awkward, their pictures mawkish and their attitudes stilted. At another, more significant, level, they have been criticized for getting in the way of real teaching, since reading schemes can be used as a substitute for individual attention. Many projects have shown how absurd it is to assume that for a teacher very occasionally to listen to children read out loud a few pages from a book will contribute significantly to their reading progress. This practice does not help; but the 'hearing' of reading persists, since it is the one formula implied by the use of reading schemes.

Another potentially damaging effect of over-reliance on reading schemes is that they become associated with the difficulties of being confronted with a text that is either meaningless and off-putting, or so dull that reading becomes a chore. The fluent reader who is made to go through a Scheme's Book One 'because that is the stage she is supposed to be at', has not even the satisfaction of an interesting story. There was a time when the idea of reading was so strictly controlled that children were made to plod through the most inappropriate material. There are many stories of children who are relatively advanced readers being given 'infantile' texts since that is all the school can offer.

Most children, of course, learn to read in their own secret ways, and learn *despite* the barriers unwillingly set up against them. Long before the 'stage' of 'book one', children can learn to follow the idea of reading, enjoy sharing a book with their parents, and intelligently work out how words are read. Children will survive all kinds of problems, but this does not mean that being confronted by a reading scheme, by itself, is at all helpful. The proper use of a scheme of 'graded' readers depends on the supplementary material, which is often provided, and on the teacher's willingness to understand the skills of reading. At best a reading scheme is a useful collection of interesting stories, designed to give children confidence and pleasure in what they already know. At worst it is a way of making children associate reading with drudgery.

It is a well-known and much-lamented fact that the older children get, the less they generally read for pleasure. For many children, reading a story is seen not as one of the pleasures of life, but a task to be undergone at school. As children have more control over their free time and as they need to read books for the information they contain, their love of reading, even if it was ever really there, disappears. All that is left, in contrast to the burden of the carefully graded reading schemes, is the pleasure in those texts, especially periodicals, that make few demands. It is as if children quickly turn from the texts provided to them at the beginning to those which are most easily available, most generally popular, and which provide the simplest means of conveying suspense. Reading schemes therefore do not succeed in doing what they set out to achieve. They are a very clumsy way of teaching the discriminations of reading, and they do not give children a lasting sense of the pleasure of stories. At the beginning they are both demanding and hardly worth reading in themselves; later they do not provide the experience of reading that children need.

Many of the limitations of reading schemes are too obvious to repeat here; many of these limitations, exemplified in sentences such as 'See, Janet, see', 'Dora has Jane', 'Peter had the dog', and 'Run, Nip, run', are overcome in more recent schemes. It is nevertheless clear that there are dramatic variations *between* the different texts; they are more varied than can be explained by their using method 'd' or method 'b'. Many publishers clearly work in isolation from reading researchers and the teachers of reading. Furthermore, books written for early readers tend to use more and more simplified language. Nowhere is this tendency to avoid the complex and demanding more apparent than in some modern versions of fairy tales. Both the story and the language are emasculated; in place of demanding or difficult concepts and vocabulary, children are given the simplified and naïve.

Children learn very complex concepts when they are very young; they can apply their minds to tasks which, although we later take them for granted, are understood only through the application of very careful thought. When children read stories they are similarly willing to work at the meanings, to explore new words. The fact that many of their mistakes are based on their inner responses to the text and intelligent guesses shows how closely involved they can be with what they read. Given that interest, nothing is harder to read for adult or child, than 'I can fan a sad man'.

For many children who are given the earliest reading books, which are no more interesting or demanding than a series of flash cards, reading becomes an experience totally at odds with any suggestion of pleasure or purpose. Primary-school children consistently discriminate between valuing reading and enjoying it. It is known that those children who do read prefer doing so at home rather than at school, but that only half of those surveyed refer to gaining any pleasure. They have difficulty in finding suitable books to read, and resent the fact that they might have to think and write about a book after reading it. The gap between reading for pleasure and reading for a purpose is clearly a large one. Much of this distaste for reading can be laid on the way in which reading schemes are presented. Reading schemes can give a hidden message that reading is a marginal activity, certainly not very functional, highly school-based, and not particularly pleasurable: all the attributes of a low-status activity.

The question remains whether reading schemes and literacy hours, with all their supporting material, can be a useful part of children's development of reading. It is important to make a distinction between a scheme in itself, designed as a complete package for early readers onwards, and the use of graded readers, probably graded by the teacher, designed to be appropriate to the level of interest displayed by the children. The most successful system of grading is based not just on vocabulary, or length of sentences, but on the content of the story, and the way a story can reflect the temperament of the child.

Reading for pleasure is a different type of activity from reading a text to prove that it has been read. Children should want to read by themselves, should be encouraged to do so, and be allowed to do so, for sustained periods of time. Too much is sometimes made of the verbal level of the text, when children are, in fact, willing to overcome difficulties if the book is interesting enough. Really good stories appeal to children of all ages, and are written in such a way that anyone who reads them can appreciate their style. The idea of 'grading' can be useful in as far as children wish to develop confidence in their reading, and need to be accustomed to the pleasure that reading can give. Children's confidence is supported by finding that they can read books easily, by acquiring a taste for reading that makes them seek out more interesting and demanding books.

In this development of children's taste, nothing is more important than the enthusiasm of the parents and the teacher. If the teachers themselves do not read, and have no particular pleasure in books, the children will soon realize it. If teachers do not continually keep up with the books that are available, they will find themselves handicapped. The ability to set out all the available texts and to know what is on the market depends on sustained curiosity. In the shortage of time available teachers are naturally inclined to trust old faithfuls, which is why the same book is being read in so many classrooms at this very minute. This trust of the well known comes about not so much from well-tested experience as from ignorance about alternatives. This is why the reading schemes, with colour coding according to levels of difficulty, seem such a ready-made solution. The fact that children will read certain books does not mean that these are the best available. Children will read a lot that bores them, and may begin to assume that reading consists of boredom.

In a more ideal world teachers would have time to explore the available literature, and match the individual personalities of the children to the books that they would most enjoy. But given the time it takes to create a system of codes (usually colours) that signifies the different levels of demands in the story – length, density of syntax, ambiguity of content – the teacher might well turn to the many available lists of graded books available. An increasing number of booklets are being published and promoted, giving titles, an indication of their content, and the level of difficulty. Although it is very rare to find anything written about the children's responses, these lists are useful reminders of what teachers can test out for themselves. Teachers can, in a sense, use graded books as part of their own stock of readers, and can also use the supplementary materials that reading schemes provide, and without which the argument behind the reading schemes is lost. In addition to the booklets, and the many stories available, it is possible to supplement conventional books with an increasing number of 'talking book' tapes that are on the market. This technique of allying the reading material with listening is an extension of the earlier recommendation to give children confidence in their own abilities to read.

Readability

Cutting through the whole question of graded readers, and the question of development beyond the earliest stages of reading, is the ambiguous concept of 'readability'. It has already been said that children can extend their abilities far beyond the norms of particular ages: the development is not a simple matter of fitting particular criteria at particular ages. Readability is a technique designed to help the grading of texts by a system of measurement. One readability graph measures vocabulary and sentence length by making a correlation between the number of syllables and the number of sentences per hundred words. Another formula divides the average sentence length by the number of words with more than three syllables. Yet another graph relies on simply adding up the number of words with more than three syllables. One type of readability formula is a vocabulary analysis. Cloze procedure has also been used for the purpose of measuring readability. In addition to these mechanical ways of measuring one text against another, there are many other factors that make books different from each other in their appeal. The layout, the illustrations and the accessibility to children: all are factors in the readability of the text. But the most important factor of all is the individual child, and the interest that child brings to the text.

The problem with readability measures is the assumption that the difficulty of a passage can be accounted for by its length and the length of sentences in it. These are simple mechanical means of measurement, they can be applied by anyone (although they all take time), and since they do not demand that the text is actually *read*, they are ostensibly objective. But they miss that side of reading that is concerned not just with decoding complex words but with understanding their uses. Readability scales assume that no one 'eschews persiflage'. The complexity of a word like 'myth' depends not on its length but on its uses. 'Antidisestablishmentarianism' might be famously long but gives little trouble in the context in which it is used (if it *is* still used, except as an illustration). 'Readability' does not assess the response on which reading depends. The most effective means of teaching the ability to read complex sentences is to teach an interest in ideas. The concept of 'readability' does not address the demands of a poem as simple in language and complex in thought as one by Blake or Yeats.

Readability measures can be used to give a comparison between texts, although it is difficult to understand why reading the text should not be just as effective a means, considering the time that a readability test takes. There is no connection between readability tests and actual difficulty. There is a distinction between the difficulty of a text and the difficulty for a reader. Readability formulae measure linguistic texts quite apart from the reader. The limitations of objective measures are clear: they fail to show, for example, how and why children read most easily those sentence structures that they themselves would write. It is, perhaps, unfortunate that the art of reading is too subtle to be contained in any simple technique like a word-count. At the first stages of reading children need to isolate particular problems so they can overcome them. At the stage at which readability measures tend to be used they are no longer appropriate. The better the reader, the easier it is to get better still. There is a curvilinear relationship between reading ability and text difficulty: once readers know what they are doing they will not find it hard to understand increasingly demanding texts.

The use of organized literacy hours

The delight children feel about stories reflects the importance they hold in their lives. Children's natural curiosity and their desire to see the world reflected in a clearly organized way make books continually important, whether they are listened to or read. As children become older they are more conscious of the stories and the way they are written: they begin to develop their own awareness of different levels in books. The need to see some mirror held up to their world continues. But between the early stories children listen to, and the later ones they read for themselves, lies a difficult gap. The problem is to provide the kind of material that satisfies their needs as well as meeting their capacities. If we could provide stories of a high level of sophistication in terms of structure, detail and idea, and yet simple in terms of language, some of our problems would certainly be diminished. Obviously, the fact that the mental development of children is semantically in advance of their ability to read is crucial. When a child has not learnt to read and we are trying to find some 'remedial' books, simple to read but interesting in their content, or at least about subject matter that a child is interested in, we have great difficulty in finding them. Our problem is not just that these books are not easily available, or few and far between, but that at this stage children have already been put off the idea of reading because of the dullness of what is offered to them.

Used by themselves, programmes of any kind do not really advance the child's ability to read. That children make up for this in their own, different ways proves more about children's capacity than the scheme's success. Although some schemes are clearly preferable to others, and although one can argue the case for their attempted juxtaposition of 'phonics' and 'look and say', schemes in children's early stages (they appear more attractive to children who have not yet begun to read) can confront them with an immediate association of school with a ritual labour, of being tested on what they are supposed to enjoy. Nevertheless, these intervention programmes do exist and probably will continue to do so. They appear in bundles in every school. Since they provide material that *can* be used, the question is how they can best be used. Confrontation between child and book is no help, but an adaptation of reading schemes by the teacher in a variety of different ways can transform the dull into an additional aid in the subtle art of teaching reading.

One of the most obvious ways in which a teacher can enhance the simple stories of the schemes is by asking the children to expand on them by imagining a more interesting tale, both from the pictures and from the basic story. The reading book can become the beginning of a more general exploration, a starting point rather than a test. Children can discuss the various illustrations, saying which ones they like, and seeing if they demonstrate a close relationship to the text. They can be encouraged to ask questions about the story, what the characters in it might be like and what might happen next. This discussion of the story can be related to their own experience, or related to what they know about the figures that appear. Children can be asked to bring their own pictures, which seem to them to approximate to the story, not as exact illustrations, and see which parts of the text have been pictured. The teacher can talk through the story; can expand on it, can use it as a starting point for much further development, making it interesting as it can rarely be by itself.

Children's ability to retell the story in their own words gives a purpose and extra dimension to the original text. They can make up their own version for other children. When children read books that are 'beneath their level' they can do so knowing beforehand that doing so will be a useful contrast to the more practised art of using their ability to predict. For this reason we should not worry whether children read *every* word correctly when they are reading through; it is more important for them to understand the complete story. We need to take the story whole, rather than one page at a time, and when we have done that we can go over the single pages. The story never needs to be used as a test. It should be the starting point for discussion, for pleasure and for stimulation.

Children can learn to retell the story in their own words and then compare their version, with their own inventions, to the original. One means of starting a fresh approach to reading texts is to give the children the words first, to make sure that they can read them and have seen them used, and then to let them read the story. Children can choose a particular part of the story that they like and read and talk about that. This can lead them to give their opinion of the story, to develop preferences, to pursue their own tastes. Alternatively, the teacher can ask children to find a part of the story, to point out on which page an action happens, and read that. One of the most difficult things, after all, is for children to find their place in the sequence, by making sense of the whole story (rather than responding to the end of the teacher's finger). Children can also think of an alternative ending, or a different development of the story.

Children helping each other

Sometimes the most useful help that children ever receive is from each other. We tend to ignore the 'hidden' curriculum of concern for others, perhaps because it reminds us too much of the idea of monitors. But children can be as good to each other as they can be cruel, and often have clearer insights into each other's problems than we as teachers have. The need to help each other often makes them attend more carefully to their own concerns. From a very early age children are adaptable to others, able to learn how to form relationships and spend time in working out what the needs of others consist of, as well as their own. Four-year-olds, for example, can adapt their speech to accommodate two-year-olds when they are with them. Children's abilities to interpret information for each other and to play roles are highly developed. When confronted with a task that makes sense to them, children can adapt their behaviour in an intelligent and helpful way.

This ability of children to help each other is worth using, since so many reading tasks can be shared, and since the individual children gain from having to explain as well as listen. Children are also aware of the different kinds of language code used according to the particular groups that they are in, and therefore have more insight into the linguistic expectations with which they approach a text. From explanation of the idiosyncrasies of spelling, and hearing each other read, to sharing their tastes in books, children are themselves one of the most useful resources for developing fluency in reading. All the individual attention, which is the teacher's ideal, can be organized through children helping each other with the tasks of reading.

The use of drama

The lack of verbal excitement in some of the reading schemes can be mitigated by their relationship to the richer experience of children. It could be said that any text depends upon what the reader brings to it. One of the most satisfactory ways of extending interest in a text, by relating it to other forms of communication, is the use of drama. Using non-verbal communication helps children understand the importance of words; the difficulties of explaining through gesture shows how much we rely on clearly written as well as spoken instructions. In a game called 'crambo' one child says what he thinks of a word that rhymes with (say) 'ball'. Other children in turn mime what they think is the right word, until they get the right one. 'Charades' can be used to draw attention to the use of syllables in words. Children can also construct short pantomimes around familiar themes.

Even the most banal of games can be enhanced by parody. It is always a temptation to cite some of the more ludicrous aspects of a formal reading scheme by placing them out of context. Children can use parody as a direct form of drama. Just as they can easily parody television advertisements, or teachers, so they can use this talent by making something out of what they read. The sense, the value, of dialogue is enhanced by its use in drama. This can be done through puppets as well as the enacting of short scenes. Models of the scenery can be made, and dramatic reconstructions of parts of the story can be planned and written out. Although much of this kind of work will take place in groups, it is also possible for individual children to work out a version of a scene in a reading book, designing it to be played by actors.

Intervention schemes are not only an end in themselves. They can be a starting point for many other activities through which children learn to adapt and extend their reading.

Chapter 16
Particular problems in learning to read

Dyslexia and reading difficulties

We sometimes forget how difficult some children find the initial stages of reading. We are therefore tempted to ignore the difficulty. Something that appears to be so obvious to us, and which causes such difficulties in others, is at the heart of the dilemmas of teaching. Where does one begin to diagnose and explain? So much learning is instinctive that instructions, even the clearest of explanations, can pass the pupil by. Learning to read has its distinct problems. It is an analogy for learning generally, since the process is not so much a steady accumulation of facts and ideas as the learning of discrimination, between clues that are significant and those that are not. Learning and knowing what not to learn have a close and ambiguous relationship. Often, learning not to learn is a result.

No one knows exactly how or why the individual finds a means of understanding how to read. We know a lot about the constant problems in learning to read, as we know a lot about cognition. Yet every individual is an individual case and the same rules do not necessarily apply to everyone. The complexities are so many, arising from auditory or visual discriminations, conceptual grasps, the ability to categorize, and even sheer confidence and memory, that there is no one simple explanation. Some of the difficulties of reading are such that far too many people cannot read at all, as well as an even larger number who cannot, for want of practice, read demanding texts. Some of those adults who cannot read have specific difficulties, but many have never had or wanted the complete chance or encouragement to learn.

The term 'dyslexia' has become useful because it draws attention to the fact that difficulties in learning to read cannot simply be attributed to brute stupidity. The term 'dyslexia' has received widespread usage because it draws attention to a particular form of 'retardation', when a child of normal gifts and inclination, or even unusual gifts, finds reading a particular stumbling block for a long time. Partly because children who were unable to read fluently had been labelled backward, much to the chagrin of their parents, and partly because attention needed to be drawn to all the particular perceptual techniques involved in reading, dyslexia became, one might almost say, a fashionable concept. Nowadays, however, dyslexia is taken more as a symptom of difficulties, the causes of which can be either biological or environmental, or both.

Usually, the term refers to physical problems rather than the environmental circumstances. There are at least three categories of dyslexia, the first to do with visual/spatial difficulties, the second to do with correlating and synthesizing difficulties, and the third with 'dysphasic' difficulties. The first is shown in a tendency to reverse letters, the second in difficulty in building words, and the third in the difficulty of understanding meanings, since small words are omitted. The moment these symptoms of dyslexia are pointed out we see how close they are to the more everyday problems of reading experienced by so many. There are some children who have such neurological problems that the typical difficulties of reading will always overcome them, but they are a small proportion compared to those who overcome the difficulties. All children can benefit from careful teaching; many children have a 'specific learning difficulty', problems of speech and language sequence that mean the art of reading remains for ever obscure. The term 'dyslexia' indicates that there are other paralinguistic problems undermining the ability to read. The symptoms of the difficulties are, however, very similar.

There is a relationship between reading disability and some measures of laterality, the width of vision, although the great majority of children with laterality problems have no great difficulty with reading. Far more undermining to the process of reading is the lack of a more general linguistic background. The lack of understanding is often associated with a lack of literacy at home, as well as a general cognitive vagueness. Reading obviously has its basis in the knowledge and use of language, the ability to speak and hear, and awareness of what the written form of communication is for. Many children who have reading difficulties have to make up for the lack of verbal fluency. Very few in comparison have difficulties because of the problems usually referred to as 'dyslexia'. All cases, however, need to be helped in very similar ways by a clear indication of the peculiarities of script, as well as the encouragement to use language and develop perception.

Unfortunately for the teachers of backward readers, there is no evidence, in all the research, that there is any single cause of reading difficulty, or any single solution. It is, however, clear that most difficulties that children have are with the recognition of blends and words, rather than with individual letters or sentences, and that the knowledge of accurate pronunciation helps children in their reading. It is also established that the most useful remedial help for children is the same as the first stages of learning: that they need to go through an understanding of auditory and visual discrimination, and their application to an understanding of blends and words. The reading tasks we set the slow reader are not that different from techniques used for the first stages of reading.

Many of the difficulties of reading have been blamed on the peculiarities of the orthography of the English language. The alphabet system might have particular difficulties compared to either logographics or syllabic systems. But given that the alphabetic nature of English needs to be understood, the English system is not, in fact, that difficult or inconsistent. Its complexity lies, oddly enough, in the fact that there are many consistent rules, as well as a few exceptions. Children, by their own rule-making behaviour, are soon aware of the alternatives, of mismatch, of things that do not fit. There is no evidence that children resort to 'sounding' what they see. On the contrary, they show an ability to learn spellings systematically. They acquire an awareness of the nature of English words, rather than random letter sequences. They realize the problems of the inconsistencies as fast as they understand the consistent rules that govern the language.

Spelling

A girl of six was asked by a visitor to her school what she would like to be when she grew up. Her reply reflected the confidence with which she perceived the prevailing attitudes: 'I want to be a speller'. There might not be any palpable reward for those who are good at spelling, but those who find it difficult are often punished. Those who like to criticize the education system find evidence of pupils' inability to spell particularly satisfying. Spelling is not a separate problem but one inextricably linked to reading. The ability, or inability, to spell reflects the way in which one has been taught to read. The same skills and perceptions are involved: the connection of sound and shape, the understanding of the construction of words, and the speed and precision of associations.

It is always possible to do tricks with the spelling system, by putting together unnatural sequences of unusual exceptions, for example:

ghoughteightough	=	potato
ppgelong	=	spelling
ghoti	=	fish

But this game actually shows up more clearly how familiar are the exceptions in their context. Much more to the point is the example of how uncomfortable it is to read a sentence when the semantic knowledge contradicts the conventions of spelling:

When they herd bear feat in the haul the bouy tolled hymn he had scene a none.

Homonyms like pale and pail, plane and plain reveal, when one analyses their roots, that many of the different spellings are based on semantic distinctions. The writing system is itself a convention in which left to right sequence, following the order in which words are spoken, and correspondence of shape to sound, are all accepted.

The rules of spelling

As well as the essential conventions of the system, there are a number of firm rules that are consistent. The 'q' is always followed by 'u'; 'y' not 'i' appears at the end of words; " before 'e' except after 'c'; the 'e' must be knocked off before 'ing'; the consonant is doubled before 'ing'; at the end of a short word the 'l' 'f' or 's' is doubled; no word ends in 'v' (apart from 'spiv'); the 'k' sound after short vowels is written 'ck', and the final 'e' is dropped before adding an ending beginning with a vowel, but kept before a consonant, eg love, loving, lovely, rattle, rattling, rattled; drive, driving, driver. Most of the spelling system is so consistent that one needs no rules to explain it; consonants are consistent nearly 100 per cent of the time; even vowels fall more into the categories of the usual than the exceptional.

The children who can spell tend to do so by learning the rules and applying them, rather than through learning by rote. But more importantly, they are aware of the ways in which words are put together. They listen carefully and look closely, until they are accustomed to the fluency of reading. Obviously no child will learn to read merely by knowing a set of rules. The skill of reading still remains that of understanding the idea, the way in which letters blend. In a sense there is no such thing as a silent 'e' since it influences the rest of the word. Children need to see that the correspondence between a sequence of sounds and a sequence of letters is appropriate, as in 'same' or 'time'. Many of the difficulties children have with spelling come about not because of the inconsistency between a letter and a sound, but because they have not yet learnt to have the confidence to blend letters, to see the words whole. The expectation that *every* letter will equal an exact sound, in a rigid sequence, causes the despairing labour of trying to sound out words. The techniques of spelling and the techniques of reading are very close.

Children's instinctive desire for consistency and their ability to map out structures are shown not only in the mistakes they make in reading but in the mistakes they make in writing. They do not make random choices but, even if independent of the adult system, make consistent phonological judgements. The pattern of errors for children who make reading and spelling mistakes is different from those who only have problems with spelling. In the latter case the children have difficulty in the perception and recall of letter groupings. In the former case the children make more phonetic errors.

Although reading and writing soon turn into the ability to decode with such fluency that it almost does not seem like thinking, spelling requires absolute accuracy as well as speed. The types of mistake readily made often derive from either not listening very carefully to a word or else not looking very carefully at it. The fact that so much language is mainly heard rather than seen, and then only half-heard, makes accurate spelling the more difficult. When some children were being asked to write about their interests more than 1000 wrote about their favourite programme on television, but it took about 150 different spellings to communicate which programmes they preferred. They had often heard the names, and talked about them, but had never looked closely at the way they are written. Very young children are liable to be inaccurate, and create a version of the correct spelling which bears the same relationship to the original word as 'kwik' or 'nite' in the names of products.

It is sometimes felt that spelling is a separate problem from reading, but the fact that children have specific difficulties of a consistent kind shows that the arbitrariness of some of the rules of spelling makes reading more difficult for them. It is almost impossible to separate fluent reading from writing. Reading depends on understanding the slight idiosyncrasies of our spelling system. One can argue that reading is altogether an arbitrary process, since each language has different sound/sense correspondences; it certainly seems like this to a child. And yet, for all the individual inconsistencies, there are a few basic realizations that need to be understood, and if a child can internalize these the rest comes comparatively easily.

Many, if not all, of the mistakes that children make (that are not a matter of refusing to think, or emotionally withdrawing from the problem) depend on one main factor, that of making a general approximation towards a specific clue. One version is to over-generalize a rule, and the other is to make a rule too specific. Thus when children are learning language they might call a favourite toy a 'car', but not a picture of a car, or a real car. The child will associate the word with just one object. On the other hand the child might over-generalize by thinking that 'car' refers to anything that moves on four wheels. In reading, the problem is the same. Having seen that some digraphs blend easily, children will suddenly find that they do not signify the same sound. On the other hand they will sometimes recognize a letter or blend in one context but not in another because they are not transferring the rule.

Children need to internalize their reading so that they know when to apply consistent expectations and when not to. When we look at any word long enough it looks absurd. We often wonder if we have spelt a word correctly, and the longer we wonder about it the less sure we are. The same is true for children as they learn to read: the more they consciously try to impose sense on a word, the less sense it appears to make. While it is necessary to concentrate occasionally on specific problems, they are really only illustrations of the more general problems in reading, and cannot completely be isolated. Any solution to children's reading difficulties includes the need for confidence, and the knowledge of those things a child can do, such as make visual discriminations and use language orally. It is more fruitful to concentrate on these things than on the specific problem of what they cannot do, like a fluent reader looking too long at the same word.

One of the simplest reading problems, which is not overcome just by concentration, is that of letter reversals. The most obvious example is the confusion between 'b' and 'd'. One way to help overcome this is to concentrate on drawings or shapes that can be changed according to left or right; in other words, to concentrate once again on shape and the left to right orientation. For the confusion is not just over the two letters that seem similar; it often covers other reversals (say of digraphs) as well.

The other way to help is to talk clearly about the difference between the letters and put them repeatedly into words, so that they are not just seen in isolation. The distinction between 'drums' and 'ball' is easier to learn than that between 'd' and 'b' in isolation. It is sometimes useful to emphasize the difference by some simple mnemonic device such as associating the 'b' with a word like 'beat', and 'd' with drag, so that there is some other level of ideas that the child can hold to.

There is always a tendency for children to confuse letters with similar features or reversible parts, such as 'p' and 'q', 'h' and 'n'. Once children have enough knowledge of more distinct letters, so that the more confusable ones can be given a context and a use, then any number of games drawing attention to the difference will help, provided that the letters are not just left as isolated symbols. If a card with either 'd' or 'b' is held up, it is noticeable that a child will make the same mistake again and again. A letter that is confusing needs a context. Although one should begin by giving children a firm base before the possible confusions are sorted out, it is not a bad thing to draw attention to possible difficulties, rather than ignore them. We can afford to take children into our confidence, and ask them to do an experiment to see which letters can be turned back to front and still remain the same, such as 'm' and 'w'.

Visual confusions are an initial form of difficulty; later problems tend to arise because of the difficulties in connecting sounds to letters. This is particularly summed up in two problems that children often face: the final 'e' and the reading of the letter 'r' at the end of a word. The problem with the hidden 'e' is that it retrospectively changes the sound and meaning of a word. It is the first introduction to children of the importance of scanning, of knowing what will come next beyond a digraph. There is no easy way of explaining this rule except by constant demonstration of blends: for example, by contrasting 'hat' and 'hate', 'dot' and 'dote'. Children can find their own list of words that conform to the same rule, even if it means making up nonsense words. They can be given a series of words and asked which of them can be changed, with meaning, by adding an 'e'. The distinction between the two types of word can be underlined by making up sentences orally, leaving out one word, and asking children which of two alternatives – say, 'hat' or 'hate' – could fit into the natural meaning of the sentence.

The final 'e' is a difficulty because it makes a crucial difference to the sound and meaning of the whole word. The opposite type of difficulty children have is when certain letters make no difference to the sound of the word and yet are a part of their spelling. The 'h' in 'when', and the 'w' in 'write', are redundant letters, which attention needs to be drawn, either by establishing a common 'code' (ie all the words that start with wh) or else by drawing out the contrast of other words that sound the same but are written differently. One way to approach this is through what is sometimes called the 'schwa' sound: the 'e' in 'the'. This particular sound has no particular identity and yet it recurs again and again, being spelt in no less than 18 different forms. It is with problems of this kind that a simplified form of diacritical marking can be very useful, provided that the teacher concentrates on one particular problem at a time.

The other common difficulty children have is with 'r' as in 'girl' or 'bar', partly because the letter does not have a strong sound value in that context (although it does elsewhere), and partly because it changes the way in which the word would otherwise be sounded; it is another retrospective change. It is worth concentrating on it in words like 'arm', 'carve' and 'park' as a specific phenomenon. Many of these specific difficulties are symbols of the common problems that children face.

Children need to learn to apply rules rather than know them by rote. We can draw attention to peculiarities such as the fact that the same sound can be written in two different ways, for example keep/cup, king/cat. The more aware children are of these obvious inconsistencies, the more they will see the secret of reading: the ability to interpret clues, rather than merely respond to them, and to interpret them so naturally that it becomes an automatic response.

Just as the same sounds and different spellings can be treated together, so can vowel clusters, using single vowel clusters such as those in 'boat', 'seat' and 'fail', then double ones, with vowels and consonants, as in 'beach', 'steal' and 'beast'.

The concentration on a particular sound in a variety of spellings can help children clarify one difficulty. This goes not only for single letters and digraphs but for other parts of words used in a variety of different ways, for example 'cure', 'secure' and 'curious'.

All these ideas stress the importance of maintaining a balance between particular difficulties and the more general context in which they fit. Diacritical marking can draw attention to the specific in the middle or the general by having a set of fixed symbols such as 'v' = silent and 'a' = stressed. Rather than create a whole series of extra marks for children to read, which can become as complex as when every single phoneme (there are 44) has its own distinctive colour, it is better to concentrate on one problem at a time. We can use the colour green to emphasize the variety of spellings used to denote one individual sound, as in 'key', 'receive' and 'bead'. Once children have understood a new point, like the silent 'e', then we should not need to continue drawing attention to it by putting a circle round it.

One of the misunderstandings about spelling, which deserves pointing out again, is based on an over-simple conception about how children learn. Some teachers suggest that if children are allowed to experiment, to invent 'false' spellings for certain words, they will be corrupted for life. With a perfect belief that children learn everything they see, these teachers feel that a child should *never* be allowed even to glance at anything but 'correct' spelling, never mind think about it. If children did learn in such a simplistic way, all our troubles would be over; we could mould them for life, with all the 'correct' responses. But learning is never so simple. The judgement and discrimination of a child is involved from the start, even before the 'right' and 'wrong'.

It has been suggested that accurate spelling can be fostered by a knowledge of the history of the language, in its gradual change. This is half true: only half, because it would be far too sophisticated an enterprise to undertake with children. An understanding of morphemes, however, comes before children are aware of what a 'morpheme' is: an insight into the ways in which words are put together, through syllables. Small units of meaning, like the 's' of the plural, support knowledge of the background of words. Just as children need to be told how to use and spell contractions such as 'I'm', 'I'll', 'I've', 'can't' and 'don't' through an understanding of the longer form, so they need to learn the ways in which all words are put together in terms of a series of conventions. It is never possible to separate the meaning of a word from its sound, for many mistakes in spelling are made by a substitution of the right kind of rule in the wrong place, like 'howse' for 'house'. This example also shows the slightly inaccurate auditory difference that causes many mistakes.

It is essentially through an understanding of syllables that an ability to spell is fostered, an understanding that needs to be encouraged by the *use* of words in context, rather than a weekly spelling test of arbitrary words. The units of words when put together, like:

care full y

help clarify the right spelling in a way no other analysis can do. Thus the teaching of prefixes and suffixes like 'dis' or 'mis' helps put right a large number of spelling mistakes, for children can again see how the words are made up. Suffixes such as 'ful', 'ly', and 'ing' also need special attention so that children know when to put in the 'e', as in 'lovely', or not as in 'mak e ing'.

It is always best to concentrate on particular mistakes often made, rather than on *every* one in a piece of written work. There are certain common problems in spelling, as in reading, which not only come up often, but if put right can lead to the resolution of other mistakes as well. There are reasons why these following cases cause difficulty: they draw attention to some of the peculiarities of the language. One common difficulty is the change from 'y' to 'ies', for example, 'party' to 'parties'. The explanation of this change draws attention to the different parts of the words, and shows how one case can apply to several words. A second difficulty is the question of the double letter, which shows the difference in pronunciation between stressed and unstressed syllables, as in:

'fury'   and   'furry'
'later'   and   'latter'

Some of the rules of English have become so natural that we overlook their derivation, as in the difference in pronunciation between 'linger' and 'singer'. When you think about where they come from, the distinction is clear.

The third significant difficulty comes from the lack of clarity in some unstressed syllables: the sound 'er' causes mistakes since it is spelt differently in words such as 'butter', 'similar' and 'colour'. A reliance on nothing but phonics is clearly never enough; in fact it is one of the reasons why young children (and semi-literate adults) find it so hard to spell.

There are a large number of enjoyable games that can help the teaching of spelling. A useful aid in many of them is, of course, a dictionary, which should be used as early as possible. However simple the dictionary, it is often more useful to have one than a personally collected list of words. To look up a word in a dictionary implies the knowledge of where to look, and the rules of how a word works. This kind of rule can be learnt, and discussed, by asking children to spell nonsense words like 'slithy' or 'frimble'; through this they see the *possible* rules, without being too overwhelmed by the fear of getting it wrong. Teachers can also ask them to pronounce nonsense words they have written out. It is always interesting how often there is common agreement on how a word would be spoken or written. Some simple games are particularly useful in spelling; children can play 'hangman' or 'Shannon's' games, in which, after the initial letter or two, the child is not just guessing in an arbitrary manner but needing to know what is likely to come next for example, from:

t h _ _ _ _ _

to

t h i m b _ _

Children can also be asked to write words that start with the letter that the word before ended with: from 'lamp' to 'part' to 'tank' to 'king'. They can also be asked to create new words that contain the letters of the old word, such as from 'old' to 'bold'. One game which can be taken at a simple or a sophisticated level depends on attempting to avoid spelling a complete word for as long as possible. If there are two teams, one will suggest a letter like 'd'. If the other team suggest 'o' they have lost since 'do' is a word; the idea is not to let the word end. But either team can challenge the other to make sure that they are thinking of a real word and not just a series of letters. A dictionary is once again a necessary standby.

The learning of spelling comes in the end to the question of memory, and the simplest way to teach it, and learn it, is to look at a word that has been misspelt within a passage, have it pointed out, find out the correct spelling, remember it, and write it down accurately. This is the kind of relearning that children can do at home. Once there is knowledge of the word it needs to be used in context, so that the correct form is used automatically. The greatest aid to this type of memory is the understanding of particular units in a word, and the joining of syllables, for this means that there is not too much to recall at one time: usually two, three or four distinct parts, a number small enough not to tax the immediate ability of visual recognition too harshly. From the start children can be asked to look at a word, fold over the paper, and see if they can write it out correctly. The importance of memory shows how closely allied are spelling and reading; the ability to do one can help the other.

It is accepted that correct spelling is important, not just out of a sense of its symbolism for the properly 'educated' but because it is a natural extension of the ability to read. The inability to spell can be merely annoying and even affordable by those of such genius that their mind flows faster than their pens; but even these would recognize their own mistakes. Children are not being helped if spelling is ignored, not only for their own futures but because they themselves are nearly always keen to be 'good spellers', just as they like to have their own work properly presented. They like to be encouraged to go beyond the imprecise and the messy.

Children will often take extra care with their spelling if their work is used for some kind of display. This can be used by the teacher to encourage children to demonstrate overcoming particular mistakes. It is important for a teacher to admit the inconsistencies of our spelling system, as well as demonstrating, through the spelling of nonsense words, how often there are also consistencies and rules that do apply, without which English would be as hard to learn as a new ideographic script. Like reading, spelling is a mixture of match and mismatch; and it is through the recognition of this that children can most be helped.

Chapter 17
Assessment

We live in an age of assessment. The language of performance and targets, as well as detection and comparison, pervades our lives as if these means were an end in themselves. Whatever the terms employed, from testing and measurement to competition and shame, the notion of apparent transparency and openness has become so powerful that it has replaced all means of development or help. All is to be tested and measured, against ever-new targets and new standards, so that if something was not found wanting before it soon can be. Whether it is in the name of accountability or not, the obsession with measurement seems to have overtaken actual behaviour. No one would deny the importance of knowledge, of what is going on, but evaluation, that desire to both acknowledge and develop actual performance, is quite distinct from the assumption, so easily reported, that the assessment of performance is an end in itself. Creativity and development lie not in measurement, but in measures to help.

In the teaching of reading, diagnosis plays a crucial part. It is quite distinct from the various reading tests with their notions of reading ages, and generalized standards. These tests can in themselves be useful as teaching aids, but the distinction between measurement and insight into the individual is such that some researchers have suggested that even diagnosing the cause of a reading problem is futile, is irrelevant, compared to the utility of instruction. At best, diagnosis is a means of help.

The distinction between testing and diagnosis is an important one. Testing is an attempt to make some kind of terminal judgement, to compare one child to another. Diagnosis is a way of helping the individual child by finding out exactly what he or she needs to know. Many of our educational difficulties stem from the fact that testing has become more fashionable than diagnosis, even though in reading it is only true diagnosis that can help the child learn.

At first this distinction between testing and diagnosis might seem too fine a one. We can argue that we test so that we might diagnose, and that we need general diagnosis so that we can test general standards. But it is the conflicting attitude behind both which is important. Real diagnosis can make a difference: it makes demands on the teacher that go well beyond administration; it is a starting point for teaching rather than a final judgement. The teacher needs to know exactly what is going on, so that assessment is inevitably taking place every day. Testing can be separated from the functions of teaching; diagnosis never can. In an important sense, all the ideas in this book can be used as a means of diagnosis. We cannot separate the concepts of diagnosis and teaching. We need to be aware of how children are developing as much as of the standard they have reached; not only the amount of knowledge they have acquired, but their style of learning. Only then does assessment become a creative instrument.

Diagnosis depends on a knowledge of two things. The first is the learning styles of children: the different types of response and development, so that we are able to act with the subtleties and idiosyncrasies of each child. The second is an understanding of the skills involved in reading, all the different factors involved in visual and auditory responses, from psychomotor skills to sophisticated criticism. True diagnosis depends not only on these factors but on the way they blend. This is why this book as a whole could be read as a book about evaluation, or about assessment if this is the perferred term.

Every idea designed to teach a particular skill is also a diagnosis. We explore the difference between the known and unknown even while we teach. Every remark that points to a less simplistic view about child development is an attempt to encourage teachers to adopt their teaching more closely to the needs, the limitations and the gifts of every child.

If we need to diagnose individual children's difficulties, then diagnosis is itself an individual matter. Teachers all have to find their own way of recording, and this comes more readily by practice than by any superimposed testing scheme. Diagnosis is recording exactly which skills children possess, and putting these individual findings into some kind of order. It is not just a matter of seeing what mistakes children make, but a matter of understanding what children produce. Nearly

171

every piece of work reveals not only something about the skills children employ but also something about the attitudes involved. Children's work is revealing, and not adequately acknowledged by a *generalized* comment such as 'good' or 'well done', or a mark and a few 'sp's' in the margin.

Whatever we choose to say on the script, demanding a thoughtful response by the child, we should be making far more sophisticated assessments for our own purpose. There are few pieces from which we cannot learn if we apply that very ability to read closely that we are trying to teach children. Of course it takes time, and of course we know that teachers are not allowed the time to do their job properly. It is nevertheless possible to set aside certain pieces of work, if not all, for elaborate diagnosis: to look at an item again and again until we know how it was done.

With children in the earliest stages, it is worth developing the role of peripatetic teachers and parents in the classroom, to carry out some teaching while the teacher talks to individuals and records what goes on. If every mistake is noted the moment it is made, distinct patterns will be revealed, the kinds of consistent mistake that can be rectified. The reason for suggesting that a second person in the classroom can be used in this way is simply that it is difficult to talk to the child and record properly at the same time. It is only when we have taken down every mistake, and made comments, that we can reflect on the under-lying tendencies, and what to do about them. When we are marking a script we are similarly recording the bias towards a certain kind of vocabulary or sentence, as well as inventive spelling or unformed letters.

When we look closely enough, we learn what is really going on inside the child's inner world of learning. This is what helps us teach. Details of home background, peculiarities of relationships or finances – just those records which upset parents as an invasion of individual privacy – do not really help teachers. Those facts make little difference to the skills of teaching. It can be an excuse to suggest that in the face of such circumstances there is little to be done; it might at best shift an attitude towards a little more understanding and sympathy, but it does not help the teacher as much as knowing the *way* in which the individual child thinks, and how this thinking can be developed. Real diagnosis is not concerned with background, explanations or excuses, but with the individual needs of children. It is not concerned with a particular 'level' of attainment but with the desire to explore the possibilities of each child's progress.

There are one or two 'test' manuals that are useful in so far as they are diagnostic. They can be used for teaching as well as discovering the particular difficulties of each individual child. The standard reading tests are examples of this. But they give only a few suggestions about what to teach, and on what basis. The teacher can develop many more ideas to promote the same ends, from different aspects of visual and auditory memory to left to right orientation, and so on. In one respect, however, it is clear that the diagnostic tests are infinitely better than the graded tests of the Schonell type, which tested nothing more than the ability to do Schonell-type tests. With failings such as vocabulary taken out of context, and a choice of words that was idiosyncratic in the extreme, their popularity showed that administrative convenience can overcome fundamental educational needs. Tests of the Schonell type are not useful for a teacher trying to learn about the child. What is a teacher supposed to do about a child who is unable to read (the first time, anyway) a word like 'tautology'?

The important point is that assessment is not an operation whose mysteries need to be wrapped in an official form, or which needs to be in some way uniform. Instead, teachers should constantly diagnose children's abilities: not allowing an initial impression to influence their attitude, but being concerned with the children's attitudes as well as skills. The teacher needs to find some way of assessing the individual; some way of making criterion reference marks, with the criteria being different for each individual child. This is a matter of estimating exactly what the needs are, and setting up a programme from all the possible ideas that fit those needs. By concentrating on *one* weakness it is possible to make a difference, not at a stroke, but by the use of a variety of techniques. The teacher then finds that *other* weaknesses are overcome at the same time; but the correction of one palpable fault gives children increasing confidence. They then know that they are in the hands of someone who sees what they want to learn and has the means to do something about it.

The secret of helping the individual is to concentrate on one thing at a time. Always have one particular matter to check and follow up. It is easier for the teacher, and has the linked advantage that other similar mistakes will be corrected subconsciously and in passing. Overcoming one mistake gives the pupil confidence in putting right others. It is a negotiated position that demonstrates the possibility of learning. Once a simple matter is detected and put right, the inward principles of learning can be extended, and the instruction taken as support rather than threat. Nothing is more off-putting than a mass of what appears to be angry signs of dismissal of a piece of work.

Choosing one thing to concentrate upon means there is a possibility of follow-up, of sharing a personal and professional interest that is both exact and supportive. What, then, happens to all the other mistakes? The pupil must ultimately learn self-diagnosis. No amount of purely external help, if that is all that is relied upon, will help. One of the simplest techniques is therefore to point out *where* mistakes are, so that the pupil, bit by bit and without blame, can correct them until the whole passage is right. Many pupils take a particular pleasure in the guessing game of detecting the 'right' answer when it comes to those matters to be learnt, as in the outcomes of reading, where there is only one.

The evaluation of the pupil's work is based on the notion that he or she can and will learn. It is a fault in the balance of teaching and learning that this in itself would do more good than all the tests available.

Part five

Extending reading skills

'Better say nothing at all. Language is worth a thousand pounds a word!'
(Lewis Carroll, *Through the Looking Glass*, Chapter 3)

Chapter 18
The uses of literacy

We never stop learning to read. The skill of unravelling a text or a tax form is only one level of reading. The abilities to understand the implications of the text, and to understand its style and meaning, constitute the true art of reading. The awareness of the symbolic value of marks on the page is soon transformed into the knowledge of what such marks signify, so that reading is not just reading the words, but reading through them. The fluent reader is no longer conscious of the act of reading. Learning to read is not an end in itself, but the beginning of the true skill of reading.

The development of children is sometimes diminished by the assumption that reading is a skill which is learnt early, and once learnt, can be ignored. Many children are not accustomed to reading in the true sense of exploring a text. Even those who do well enough to go into higher education often find the skills of studying difficult to learn. They know little about how to organize their reading, how to analyse a text, and how to vary the pattern of their reading. Any intellectual advance, development of logic or encouragement of sensitivity, depends on reading. The written word is not only a useful means of collecting and storing information, but one demanding clarity of thought and precision of expression. In speech we communicate through conviction, and despite the redundancy of many repeated phrases. Although there are some who, either by their speed of mind or by their slowness of tongue, can match their ideas to the most elegant of sentences, most of us need the discipline of writing to work out exactly what we mean to say. Even that can be very difficult. Reading gives the chance to think about, as well as listen to, what is being said.

Reading is engaging the mind with ideas in such a way that these ideas can be scrutinized at the same time as being experienced. Reading is a discipline from which we can learn more than from the closest observation of a good film, or the most intense concentration on a lecture. Reading is a balance between the awareness that we are responding to something and the ability to make it our own. Reading goes beyond an instant response to propaganda or slogans, or sympathy for a tale of woe. Reading is a mixture of the critical and the responsive. Far from being a way of inducing the mind to an unspontaneous pattern of logic, reading helps develop a sense of personal sensitivity. It is a 'public' act that is also private; but it is one in which the difference is always apparent.

Reading is, therefore, an extension of the mind. It is not a passive skill through which we receive information, but an active engagement with ideas. Advanced reading implies the development of those skills which have always been inferred but rarely fostered, the ability to discriminate between what is said and the way it is expressed. The recognition of what is well or wittily expressed is only one part of the satisfaction of being continually aware of how ideas are conveyed, whether in a novel, a magazine, or an academic text.

Reading implies an awareness of the style of a text, an awareness of the 'level' of a text in terms of its demands and its designs upon the audience, and an awareness of the implicit bias of a text. Language can be used to manipulate and control as well as to clarify and explain. We learn to read so that we can understand the different uses, or styles, of language. Children need to learn how language is used, and develop the curiosity about words that shows they are aware of the different uses of language in their own lives. Just as they are good at adapting their language to each other and according to different circumstances, so they need to realize that language is always being adapted by other people in various ways.

Style is the unconscious or conscious delineation of a point of view. It reveals something about the author, and something about the author's attitude to the reader. We often read for information without stopping to look at the way it is presented. There are many instances when we are made aware of the means of communication. Advertisements are one example; propaganda is another. Once people are aware of style, they are then much better equipped to read more complex prose: we enhance the capacity to read by making children more demanding in what they read, by encouraging them to expect real rewards from their reading. We ask them to look more closely at what they read rather than control what they read.

One of the best examples of the use of language for particular purposes comes from advertisements. The syntax and vocabulary can be analysed both in terms of the intentions behind them, and in terms of that peculiar world of half-truth where nothing is quite what it says. 'Pure gold'. The language of magazine advertisements can be analysed in terms of the grammar; the spoken idiom or the overheard remark. The use of adjectives, and the underlying appeal to a particular market, can be aspects considered in comparing advertisements for similar products. The pictures themselves can be 'read' in relation to the text; the way the product is presented and its setting. The kinds of image used to enhance the product can be discussed. The tone of the text can be analysed. The famous names that endorse various products can be listed. All the occasions when the most typical phrases of advertisements are used can be noted: 'the biggest, better than . . .' Any material can be subject to analysis.

The language of advertising tends to be of a particular kind. It avoids abstractions, is based on the spoken rather than the written mode, and is the same whether it is used to describe jeans or patent medicines, banks or cigarettes. It replaces sentences with phrases. The sense of the positive, the easy to read and listen to, prevails:

'Try . . .'   'Have . . .'   'Enjoy . . .'

Words like 'because' tend to be replaced by 'That's why', and instead of complex syntax a system of endless technical pre-modifiers is used:

'Fully guaranteed hand-made luxury long-lasting . . . .'

Certain words are most used: 'new', 'good' (or 'best'), 'fresh', 'delicious', 'full', 'sure', 'natural', special'. In the English of advertising there are, in fact, not only linguistic peculiarities but also a consistent pattern of claims. Advertising can be analysed in terms of the various appeals used. The 'unfinished' claim is that which 'gives you more' (than what?). The 'empty word' claim uses the words 'helps' or 'fights' as in 'helps control dandruff'. (This implies that it does not actually stop it; a bucket of water 'helps control' forest fires.) The 'unique' claim merely suggests that: 'There's no other mascara like it' (ie the others have different names). The 'water is wet' claim suggests that the obvious is somehow different: 'The natural beer' or the 'detergent gasoline' (they all are). The 'so what' claim proffers only half the facts: when 'you get twice as many in the same packet', it means that the contents are smaller. Statistics are a favourite advertising standby; 'It has 33 per cent more cleaning power than another popular brand' (ie it is one-third larger), or 'It helps build up bodies 12 ways' (ie doesn't help in another 12). But many claims are based on deliberate vagueness, whether they are rhetorical ('Wouldn't you rather have a ...?'), compliment the consumer ('We think you are someone special'), or descend into the world of the meaningless ('Lips have never looked so luscious'; 'tastes good like a cigarette should'). The famous headline statements, which are neither true nor false since they are meaningless – 'can be taken anywhere', 'the effect is shattering' – can easily be collected.

There are countless examples of a particular use of language to be taken from advertisements. Obviously the main source for such reading will be magazines, but the literacy we are trying to teach also applies to television. We are trying to teach the ability to decode messages as well as symbols of script. The analysis of the use of fantasy within the advertisements, or the use of fear in making people buy certain products, is an important part of enabling children to become aware of things they would otherwise take too easily for granted. The use of figures, as in car advertisements – 85 mpg at a steady 56.5 mph – as well as the use of language can be made into a comparative study, so that the manipulation of fact as well as the awareness of fact can become part of children's reading abilities.

Any ambitious teacher wishes to help children read critically. All pupils' capacity to do so is natural, and they enjoy opportunities to display it, since each personal idea is valuable. The uses of criticism are not to be left to journalists or academics, but fostered in every reader. Once the critical sense is developed into the ability to analyse whatever is read, other parts of the curriculum will be far easier to manage. The simplest technique in the encouragement of a critical capacity is that of comparison. Any two versions of the same original subject reveal in their differences much of what we are trying to teach about the author's point of view, or subconscious bias. The material used for comparison can come from almost any source. We can, for example, take a newspaper story about the same event from different papers and see how much space is given to it, how many details are explained, what kind of judgement is made about it and what kind of language is used.

The simplest way to make children aware of the structure of the argument is to ask them to note down in headings what the main points are: a form of precis, which is more interesting and more useful than the stereotypical way in which precis has typically been used. The very juxtaposition of two stories allows a number of points to be made, and exercises carried out, from a list of descriptive words used to discussion of the relationship between the text and the pictures. Newspapers also exhibit different types of language according to the position of the story. There is headline language – 'Sex change killer axes two' – 'lobbyman's English' – 'Usually reliable sources suggest growing support at branch level for a leftward swing within the trade union movement' – and leader-writer's prose: 'It is earnestly to be hoped that so deplorable a development . . .'

Newspapers are an obvious source for comparisons, since they are so readily available; but similar comparisons can be made with magazines, comics or books. If one takes two detective stories, one can compare the way in which the plots are handled, how many clues we are given, how the atmosphere builds up, and how real or wooden are the characters. We can concentrate on a particular page and see whether it remains exciting out of context. The very comparison between two pieces makes it easier to see how language is used. If the passages are about a particular person – the hero in a detective story, or the main protagonist in the news – it is possible to compare differences in the way that person is described, both physically and in more general terms, and to discuss how the writer tries to influence what we to think about the person.

Comparisons are not odious. They are the basis on which a capacity for criticism can enjoyably be fostered. It does not need sophisticated techniques to look at the differences in two articles taken from printed ephemera. Some pupils are, after all, accustomed to comparing two poems on the same subject, or two descriptions of a similar type of character in different novels. The reason for starting with ephemeral material is that it is far easier to criticize and is less complex. It is also easier to parody. Most important of all, it is easier to see the distinct bias in the writer, even if the author is anonymous. An awareness that books have designs on us, attempt to persuade, cajole and change our minds, is at the heart of advanced reading; and is at the heart of any political awareness.

The bias of a magazine article can be seen in its tone; its attitude towards the reader. Is it attempting to be friendly, or exclusive? Examples in women's magazines or popular magazines explain themselves very easily. The bias of a newspaper story can be seen by the way it presents a case: we cannot expect children to be aware of a distinct political slant, but they can develop a sophisticated opinion about the way the individual presents arguments. Some political pamphlets are easy to discuss, partly because they go to such obvious extremes in bias, and partly because of the stereotyped nature of the language which is employed. Reviews of shows, whether taken from papers or written by children themselves, reveal not just obvious likes and dislikes but reasons for them. Even election pamphlets can be compared to reveal the simplicity of different points of view, and will take children beyond that fashionable cynical indifference that fosters irresponsibility. Advertisements for causes in newspapers, as well as for products, are another ready source for the analysis of bias and point of view.

The analysis of textual bias can include the translation of sentences into their true meanings, by finding instances when there is an attempt to gloss over a fact in such a way that it looks to its best advantage. This can be found particularly in propaganda and in travel brochures:

> As part of our constant effort to bring value to our holidays you will be pleased to find that due to the strength of the new relationship we have with the . . . group . . . (ie 'we have been taken over')

The analysis of a point of view can be a complex task, but there are many simple ways of carrying it out, and clear examples can be used to establish the idea. One of the most effective ways of showing how unconscious bias alters the way in which an event is seen, is to ask several children to write about the same event. The realization that each will see different things as significant is the beginning of an awareness of style. Children can also compare reviews they write about a particular programme they have seen. Afterwards they can compare the published reviews in different papers about the same play, concert or book. They can then go on to compare different newspaper accounts of the same event, spotting which elements are highlighted, which facts are ignored, and whether the attitude is sentimental or laconic. They can be asked to write three separate accounts of a person, about which there can be differences of opinion: one praising, one neutral and one condemning, each time using the same basic facts. When children are able to do this, they can analyse examples of writing where the bias is ostentatious: a write-up of a pop star in an adulatory manner, or a piece of propaganda attacking 'paper tigers'. Children can be asked to rewrite a passage changing its bias from one extreme to the other. They can also, if they do not agree with the views expressed, be asked to find any flaws in the argument, to see if its opinion is supported. These tasks should be supported with actual examples.

Behind an author's bias lies an attitude to the audience. If we talk of 'tone', people will find it difficult to define; but it is clear in most newspapers that there is a view of the readership that is distinctly their own. One can take examples from different newspapers and see what relationship they have to their readers: are they friendly or respectful, familiar or superior? The editorials in magazines can also be compared to see if they are cajoling or insistent, or merely self-advertising. Children can even be asked to picture what the author looks like, considering what kind of clothes, what kind of working environment, fit the style of person that is conveyed through the text. This simple task will itself reveal a fundamental truth about print that is often forgotten: that it is not sacrosanct but personal, written without any overwhelming authority.

Much of what is written is not carefully weighed by the author. Children can think about all the automatic associations that come into their own minds, and see if it is likely that they were also in the author's. They can also be asked to indicate instances when a different word might have been used from the one the author has chosen. This could entail rewriting the whole passage, changing it through the use of ostensible synonyms and noting the resulting differences. The same sentences can be rewritten in three different ways: just by a change of vocabulary; from the point of view of 'I', 'you' or 'he/she'; or simply from extremes of bias.

In what is known as Bertrand Russell's grammar, children can put the same state into three definitions, according to the point of view. Thus:

I am happy.   You are tipsy.   He is drunk.
I am cautious.   You are timid.   He is a coward.
I have something of the subtle fragrance of the orient. You rather overdo it, dear. She stinks.

Children can also find similar words for a particular idea and show how they would be used according to different motives, as in 'devout', 'pious' and 'sanctimonious'.

One of the simpler ways of noting automatic bias that derives from word associations is by an analysis of gendered language. Children can be asked to make a list, noting the connotations each word has, as in:

Bachelor   or   Spinster
Landlord   or   Landlady
Master   or   Mistress

Many words can be analysed in terms of associations. What is the difference between athlete and sportsman? What are the nuances of a word like 'playboy'? Dictionary definitions are rarely enough in themselves. A great deal depends on the context in which a word is used. Let the children analyse a series of generalizations, each of which is formed out of half-truths. Orwell's *1984* contains many good examples of the way in which propaganda works, as well as being a clear statement about the importance of language. Children can be asked to extend the idea of 'newspeak' to see if they can invent deliberately narrow languages, thus cutting out the possibilities of extended emotions. They can also be asked to list the most-used phrases or words in a propaganda article, from either the left or right-wing point of view. Through such a fairly simple exercise they learn about the assumptions implicit in the text. The generalized complaining against the undefined 'they' can also be parodied.

One of the revealing facts about certain points of view is the stereo-typed language that is used. We can ask children to list all the clichés that generally fill in gaps of thought, like 'you know' and 'this is it' or the personal clichés that people favour – 'actually', 'in a sense' and so on. (Many children have played a game which consists of betting on the number of times a teacher will use his or her favourite phrase in one lesson.) The verbal clichés of a particular television personality can be noted, both those used to elicit a response and those used in a subconscious manner. The jargon of a certain mode of thinking like that associated with being 'hip' can be subjected to parody. There are always certain words in vogue at a particular time.

The listing of all words used by a particular group, perhaps taking the children's peers as one group, draws attention to a use of language deliberately limited, a shared meaning exclusively understood. The noting of words more recently coined, or those especially in use at a given time, or by a small group: all these draw attention to the way language is used automatically, without any precise meaning, or with a meaning not supposed to be understood beyond a limited circle. This technique can be extended. Not only do we find a distinct vocabulary in the magazines designed for children – they can easily place the phrases of these into context – but we can explore the language of churches or the law. Some forms of jargon go beyond the temporary clichés of a time: language used in law is of a distinct type, into which simple instructions can be translated. We can parody the language of science, of the classroom, or of any circumstances close to children's own experience, for they are aware of jargon even before they are given a chance to be articulate about it.

The ability to parody is innate, and the results (like a version of an advertisement seen on television) can be simple as well as effective. Parody can also be extended: it is an inventive act, showing a close reading of the original. We can ask children to invent new euphemisms, and point out why euphemisms are used. There are many examples: 'comfort stations', 'rest rooms' and 'powder rooms' replace 'toilets', 'lavatories' and 'water closets'; the word 'old' is rejected in favour of 'senior'; the word 'sex' becomes 'adult'; 'uniform' equals 'career apparel'; and nothing is 'second hand' but 'an experienced or used item'. The changing uses of the language can also be studied: the misuse of a word like 'disinterested' as if it meant uninterested, or the gradual change of a word like 'professional', by its use in phrases such as 'professional foul' and 'professional killing'.

Verbal clichés are a starting point for an analysis of language. The best way to illustrate this is through a dissection of that perennial cliché, the word 'situation', which appears in a variety of 'ongoing reading situations'. Children can be asked to note down every time it is used, and by doing so will become aware how often it obscures meaning rather than clarifies it. Clichés like 'at this moment in time' are symptoms of a moribund language, one which is reduced to passive concepts. Clichés, as we can see in business English, are the crutch of those who do not wish to say anything too clearly. Orwell once translated:

> I returned and saw under the sun, that the race is not to the swift, nor the battle to the strong

into officialese:

> Objective consideration of contemporary phenomena compels the conclusion that success or failure in competitive activities exhibits no tendency to be commensurate with innate capacity, but that a considerable element of the unpredictable must inevitably be taken into account.

This is a comparatively mild example, but it shows how easy the technique is to apply. Any pithy phrase can be translated into a sentence that rambles from circumlocution to bathos. An aide asked an American Secretary of State for a pay increase. Using the language of official obfuscation, the Secretary of State replied, 'Because of the fluctuational predisposition of your position's productive capacity as juxtaposed to government standards it would be momentarily injudicious to advocate an increment.' The puzzled aide: 'I don't get it?' The Secretary of State: 'That's right.'

Official jargon is not the only example of such a use of language; we see the same tendencies, more sadly, used to deceive rather than improve. Analyses of the language used by the administrations of governments who are at war show how the brutal facts are covered up by words that seem devoid of any brutal intent. Spying becomes 'visual surveillance', human beings slaughtered are 'infiltration targets', and bombing is described as 'pressure actions'. In most circumlocutions there is a desire to cover up the reality of what words mean. There are many examples. A directive from the head of a large institution which, for lack of money, is about to throw a large number of people out of work, is almost invariably written in the kind of language supposed to mitigate the personal meanings of the action. It takes only a few examples of such uses of language to teach why we wish our students to be sensitive to jargon; the spotting of different clichés is not just an amusing game but has a very serious purpose.

Once the most extreme forms of the misuse of language are noted, it is simpler to analyse the same tendency used in different, less heinous forms of obfuscation. A delightful game can be played by attempting to translate the prose favoured by sociologists into a clear sentence. Cynics might suggest that this is impossible; those who wrote the original version may defend their complex language as necessary, and argue that each precise definition has a particular meaning. Whatever point of view we hold, it is still useful to take a close look at such examples, to see if there are other ways of expressing the same idea, for such a translation is the beginning of a sense of style.

One underlying weakness in such prose, and one which is very hard to overcome when the subject is itself theoretical, is the tendency to be abstract, even when the subject is not. We have a tendency to use the passive rather than the active tense, to use a vague phrase in place of a concrete instance. The desire to sum up an idea in a succinct phrase can be developed by encouraging the use of metaphors of an original kind; a fresh analogy that illustrates a particular point will help teach the ability to convey a personal idea. This is especially instructive if we are, at the same time, making lists of all those well-known clichés that begin their life as useful metaphors. 'Putting one's shoulder to the wheel' meant something to those who read it 100 years ago. An analysis of newspapers or magazines reveals how automatic the use of such phrases has become.

Everyday clichés, sometimes called 'Charlie Brown sentences', can also be a source for analysis, or parody:

Happiness is a warm puppy.
Love is not having to say you're sorry.

The possibilities of parody are many, but a teacher can do more than merely hold up a number of examples. Some indication of how various styles are learnt (and avoided) can be consciously emulated by awareness of their techniques. It is even possible to invent 'cliché machines', which are a self-generating means of constructing various phrases. There are three columns under which are listed various words. Any word in column one can be combined with any word from column two and any word from column three to create a cliché:

integrated	management	capability
systematic	policy	contingency
marvellous	felt	experience
overwhelming	real	happening
heuristic	teaching	situation

This example is very general, but it is also possible to construct cliché machines that focus on particular subject areas:

Qualifier	Area of involvement	Problem
Minimal	Brain	Disfunction
Mild	Cerebral	Damage
Minor	Neurological	Disorder
Chronic	Neurologic	Disynchronization
Diffuse	Language	Handicap
Specific	Reading	Disability
Primary	Perceptual	Retardation
Disorganized	Impulse	Impairment
Organic	Behaviour	Pathology
Clumsy	Response	Syndrome

Another way of increasing sensitivity towards phrases is to ask children to invent alternatives to well-worn phrases like 'golden mean', 'null and void' and 'the coast is clear'. Rather than just listing them, they can think of possible changes: 'the orange of one's eye', 'a picture of illness', 'tower of weakness', 'pepper of the earth', 'embarrassment of poverty', 'sweet grapes', and 'soft facts'. The very listing of different possibilities draws attention to what is usually read without thinking. Only tired minds resent the demands made by literature; but the way to keep the mind alert is not just to provide the forms of reading material that demand attention, but to look closely at whatever is read.

Chapter 19
The experience of reading

Strether's first question, when he reached the hotel, was about his friend; yet on his learning that Waymarsh was apparently not to arrive till evening he was not wholly disconcerted. A telegram from him bespeaking a room 'only if not noisy', with the answer paid, was produced for the inquirer at the office, so that the understanding that they should meet at Chester rather than at Liverpool remained to that extent sound. The same secret principle, however, that had prompted Strether not absolutely to desire Waymarsh's presence at the dock, that had led him thus to postpone for a few hours his enjoyment of it, now operated to make him feel that he could still wait without disappointment. They would dine together at the worst, and, with all respect to dear old Waymarsh – if not even, for that matter, to himself – there was little fear that in the sequel they should not see enough of each other. The principle I have just mentioned as operating had been, with the most newly-disembarked of the two men, wholly instinctive – the fruit of a sharp sense that, delightful as it would be to find himself looking, after so much separation, into his comrade's face, his business would be a trifle bungled should he simply arrange that this countenance should present itself to the rearing steamer as the first 'note', for him, of Europe. Mixed with everything was the apprehension, already, on Strether's part, that he would, at best, throughout, prove the note of Europe in quite a sufficient degree.

(Henry James, *The Ambassadors*, Chapter 1, page 1)

There is no doubt that the opening of Henry James's *The Ambassadors* is hard work for the reader, subtle in thought, convoluted in expression, and not unlike elegant talk to a shorthand secretary. And yet, on close acquaintance, the book is not only rewarding but one of the most clear and direct novels one would wish to read. Reading a good book is not an easy task, and the rewards gained are commensurate with the amount of effort one puts in. Reading literature is a habit that needs to be learnt. Unlike most habits it is not acquired by default, or lack of ambition. It is the reward for craving genuine satisfaction. The primary aim of teachers should be to pass on the love of reading through which true education comes. However many times one reads *The Ambassadors*, it becomes more fascinating each time, for it does not depend on a simple plot, is not a whodunit or a ritual exercise in the mechanical. Like all things worthwhile, an appreciation of reading needs to be learnt, and if learnt then taught, even if self-taught.

A novel like *The Ambassadors* is a good example of the art of reading. It demands close attention from the reader, is written in demanding sentences, and at the same time contains clear, and devastatingly simply expressed, home truths. Readers detect the meaning behind statements made by different characters, as well as detecting the overall intentions of the author. The reader needs to weigh each sentence in order to understand which carries most importance, reading not necessarily slowly, but with active engagement in the text. Reading is an almost automatic trait to be both consumed by, and aware of, the text. It is no diminution of the personal response that it includes a sense of criticism. No page of text is to be read in exactly the same way as another. Unlike a film, which cannot be halted, a book is art to which we bring our own scale of time. We choose how to read every time we start a book, just as we choose to read magazines or newspapers in a quite different way to that in which we read books.

The art of reading is the art of combining the personal and the critical. We do not let a text merely flow over us, nor do we ever read in such a way that we are only conscious of how the words are strung together. The idea of the academically 'pure' reading of a text, when the reader approaches it without any prior experience, knowledge or expectation, is a critical fallacy. We cannot help being personally involved, since we are conscious of what we are doing. We cannot avoid the personal, both in texts that demand more attention and in those that demand less. However much we try to concentrate only on those facets that seem to us important, like a particular fact or date, or a piece of information we are seeking, we remain engaged in the act of reading. Far from being a means of communication that belongs to a purely academic tradition, or to a past too ordered to be relevant to a culture of instant, electric responses, reading is a personal art. No two people read the same book in the same way.

If reading is itself an art, it follows that it can be applied to any text. How we read is as important as what we read. One of the fallacies about reading is that teachers should give a strict diet of materials from which no one should stray. It is more important to make sure that all books are read with close attention and the ability to discriminate. We learn to read according to our attitude rather than according to the material. The novels of Enid Blyton, which remain popular for the simple reason that they are as easy to imbibe as television serials, can themselves make useful objects of analysis. This can be done either in terms of the plot, analysing the structure of the book as a whole, or by looking at a particular character to see how he or she is characterized. Is the individual's personality conveyed entirely by descriptions of their appearance and behaviour and through their speech, or does the author explicitly tell the reader what to think about the person? We do not need to enter the peculiar psychology of Enid Blyton's stories to be aware of the assumptions on which they are based. Once expectations become greater, the same texts will not continue to satisfy us in the same way. It is not just a question of maturity that makes the simpler children's texts dull, but a question of expectation.

If it is possible to analyse pages of Enid Blyton, it is also possible to look at magazines or the Internet. They have their obvious attractions, one of which is to lend themselves to close analysis of a text that is not designed to be read in that way. A discussion of the tone of editorials reveals something of the attitude of the magazine to its readers. Articles about the past can become a tool for exploring the deliberate exploitation of nostalgia. The language of short stories that play on sentiment, or violence, can be analysed in terms of the vocabulary used; by underlining as well as discussion. The point of view expressed in advice columns is not just a starting point for debate, but a means of clarifying personal prejudices. One can compare the astrological predictions given in different papers on the same day for the same 'star sign'. All the teacher needs is the desire to foster a close analysis of a text, and some suitable texts for analysis, either chosen by him- or herself and duplicated for student use, or brought in by the pupils. The World Wide Web is a huge source of examples of language used in a variety of different ways for different purposes.

Magazines are just one source for the kind of critical analysis out of which advanced reading comes. Such critical skills can also be fostered by analysing media that are not primarily, if at all, word-oriented. Television, supposedly the arch-enemy of reading, is itself employable in the encouragement of criticism. To ask a class to predict what will happen in the next week's episode of a serial makes them look more closely at that which might otherwise pass them by. Reviewing the way in which the news is presented, and which stories are chosen as most important, can foster a closer insight which contrasts with the common habit of inattention. A reduction of a 'cops and robbers' story to a simple analysis of its plot can also be revealing.

The simplest way of all of encouraging children's capacity for criticism is through the use of parody. Copying the style of others demands an awareness, conscious or unconscious, of the elements of that style, and can be a first step in encouraging children to develop a style of their own.

There is a tendency in all children to parody their teacher's style, and this is something they do largely unconsciously, as part of an attempt to please. The analysis of work by any class that has been taught by the same person for some time invariably shows a class 'style', derived from what the teacher feels is important, reflecting what that teacher generally praises, and showing deficiencies in aspects the teacher tends to ignore. We can see one class writing reams of similes, another painstakingly using long words. Again and again researchers find that poems, for example, written by 18 different children in the same class are very similar in content, style and language. Clearly the teacher has had a very strong influence on the works, and this is not necessarily a bad thing: although it is inevitably at the expense of the individual child's creativity and insight, it shows that the children have developed an instinctive awareness of the teacher's personal style and preferences. The tendency to parody is inevitable; the desire to please goes deep. Teachers are usually quite unaware of the full extent of their influence. And yet if one watches a class of infants being asked questions, it is clear how much of their energy centres upon guessing what the teacher wants. Children learn quite naturally how to please, and to please by guessing what is expected of them. However, to leave children to pursue this course without encouraging analysis and awareness can not only limit their creative development, but turn their work into something dull and mechanical. And the alternative path of trying to force children to be 'creative' all the time also has its drawbacks. Even a genius cannot produce profound and original work day in and day out. The course I advocate here is for teachers to offer pupils a variety of different style models, and encourage them to analyse and imitate these. This provides some variety and stimulation, and does something to remove the limiting effect of the teacher's personal style and preferences.

Parody is a technique that children find interesting, and it can be applied to many forms of text. While the easiest examples to parody lie in magazines and newspapers, many styles of writing in poetry and prose reveal consistently particular approaches to the use of language. The easiest to imitate are those moments in stories that attempt to build a climax or reveal intense emotion or excitement, or 'purple patches' in poetry that suffer from an overuse of adjectives. The weakest style is always the easiest to make fun of; but even this teaches an awareness of language, which helps the reader respect what is best.

One way of making children aware of the attitudes implicit in what they are reading is to see if they can make 'instant' classifications of types of people, together with those ready definitions that come from verbal associations. They can list all the words used to characterize particular types of person. They learn through this about familiar images and the automatic uses of language. They can be asked to list the most hackneyed metaphors, and the most commonly used phrases. By doing so they learn to be aware of style, and see how an idea depends on the way in which it is expressed. It is not always helpful to separate what has been called the 'transactional' from the 'poetic'. Every text has some kind of style. Some are more individual than others, but even the anonymous civil service instruction or the impersonal holiday agent's brochure have distinct styles of their own.

The close reading of a text includes awareness of style. We have already suggested that reading is also learnt through writing, and that the two actions are, like style and content, inseparable. For this reason it is useful to try to help children be aware of their own writing. Their style will mostly develop naturally from their reading, but it is still helpful to encourage them to think of alternative means of expressing ideas. Parody might show how language is used, but we can also draw attention to matters of structure and phrasing, as well as vocabulary. One of the most helpful ways of understanding the use of tone is to make a study of bathos. Children can be asked to emulate the kind of sentence that starts with pomp and ends flatly, like Twain's famous example,

> 'the holy passion of friendship is of so sweet and steady a nature that it will last through a whole lifetime, if not asked to lend money'.

It is through the understanding of bathos that children become acquainted with irony, with different levels of insistence, and with understatement. They can learn through mimicking Swift's fierce ironies, such as 'Yesterday I saw a woman flayed and would hardly believe how much it altered her appearance for the worse'. They can write on the same event in a series of short, sharp sentences, with a minimal vocabulary, and then with a far more grandiose style. They can be asked to write a series of sentences that have the balanced decorum of 18th-century prose. And they can be asked to write a really purple passage.

Children can be asked to report an event, structuring their piece with the list of questions journalists are supposed to ask themselves: who, when, where, what, why and how? They can then compare the way in which they have followed this structure to a newspaper story, to see if this formula has been followed. They can also be asked to do what seems a simple task, but is in fact difficult: to describe a particular object and its uses – a shoe, a pen, a desk – in a new way, finding a different 'slant' to take, which makes the obvious unfamiliar. At a simple level they can be asked to finish the same sentence – for example, 'There are 12 shopping days to Christmas' – with different endings, starting with 'so', 'but', 'and', and so on.

The most important task of all in teaching an awareness of style is to compare, to see the same idea treated in different ways. There are large numbers of contrasts published every day; by reviewing some of them, children learn how bias is formed. They then become aware of the impact of a publication on the style of pieces written for it, and conscious of the alternative ways in which a passage might have been written, and become sensitive readers, able to read with that subtlety of response, critical insight and pleasure that denote someone able to read in the real sense of the word.

Practice is essential. There are two great difficulties facing children in continuing their experience of reading. One difficulty is that the literary heritage depends on a knowledge of the terms of reference which writers used, and which they assumed that their readers would share. Many university teachers find themselves in difficulties because their undergraduates do not know even the most common classical allusions; Biblical imagery, and all the religious references on which so much writing is based, are no longer understood. Even the most seemingly obvious references to culture, whether in visual or auditory form, seem to be less commonly digested. Literature does not only teach new ideas, but assumes a common heritage as well as a common language. One of the most important tasks for a teacher is to ensure that children, from an early age, are not locked away from all the terms in which people have conveyed to each other their experience of the human condition.

The second difficulty in the reading of literature arises from children's lack of experience of form and structure. The analysis of a text reveals that it has been carefully constructed, and that constraints of form are deliberately used. This is especially true of poetry, where the use of rhyme and the controlled use of rhythm is essential to conveying complex meaning. It is possible to select some free verse that children will find enjoyable, particularly humorous verse and verse containing dialogue, but it is interesting to note that although children like this form of verse for a time, they tend to go on associating poetry with the use of form, and tend to prefer rhyme. It is certainly much easier for children to write when they are aware of the possibilities of form.

There are many suggestions for books appropriate to different ages and temperaments. There are few studies, however, which give insight into children's responses to various texts, and few opportunities for them to talk about or analyse what they read. A novel or a poem is a private pleasure, but it should not be so private as to be an inarticulate one. While one would not wish to force children to make a critical judgement on every book they read – the comment might well be no more lucid than 'it was terrible' or 'I suppose it was all right' or 'terrific' – there should be opportunities to look in detail at *why* some stories are more successful than others. Children can explore what a text is like when read aloud to other people; they can compare different openings and consider what they have learnt from what they read for pleasure. The most useful judgements that children can be asked to make come from the attention paid to short passages, and comparisons between passages. Reading a novel may be a matter of entering into a different world, of escaping from everyday concerns, but readers need to bring to that world their critical skills. All children bring their own unique knowledge and awareness to bear, and are conscious of this in the act of reading.

Reading becomes more interesting to children when it is shared, although there is also a place for solitary quiet enjoyment. A class library is not just a stock of 'approved' books but a source of conversation, so that a display devoted to the 'promotion' of a particular writer can be set up by those who wish to spread their enthusiasm. Many children become fascinated with the whole process of book production, from the first moment of inspiration to the final marketing. The way in which a publisher makes the decision to publish, the way the book is costed, and its design, are all details that children like to explore. They also like to know why and how authors write their stories. Fortunately, many authors are very willing to come into schools to read from their works and to talk to children about how they went about the task of writing. A number of schemes are devoted to making it easy for teachers to invite writers to their classes. The impact of a writer is incalculable. It is surprising that more use is not made of the opportunities writers offer.

Children become engaged in the text through their awareness of how it is written and how it is produced. They can think about producing illustrations, choosing which passage is most significant. They can design alternative covers. They can produce diagrams of a book's structure or find incidents that could replace what is in the text. They can think of different endings, or alternative openings. They soon learn to appreciate what is apt in what is printed, and become the more engaged for being able to think of other ways in which matters could be expressed. It is through a sense of what is written that children begin to be aware of the possibilities of their own writing. Their own creativity comes about through their awareness of literature, and their ability to understand it.

One of the most potent influences of a good book is its use of a rich vocabulary. There are many people who do not use a vocabulary of more than 2000 words, and it is possible to 'survive' on as little as 300 words. But such a small vocabulary means that the communication of experience is much diminished. Just as young children learn words from use, and their meanings from context, so literature goes on teaching the uses, the meanings and the experience of words which, like the appreciation of the experience itself, open up the world. Literature should not be associated automatically with the use of long words for their own sake. Every opportunity to extend vocabulary, and the use of vocabulary, should emphasize the use and the context of words. The different uses of the same word, and the idiosyncrasies of language according to the circumstances in which it is used, can foster an appreciation of the distinctions between precision and jargon.

It is possible to look for words that are unusual in newspapers as well as poems, in magazines as well as novels. Children can find out when words are being used in an exaggerated or sensational way. They can, for example, be made aware of the differences in the use of the same words in novels and in newspapers, according to the syntax.

Zoo boy death trial starts

Children can also try to guess what story such a headline introduces, writing up a version and comparing theirs to the original. The ability to 'translate' the same collection of facts from one medium to another is an important part of children's developing abilities as readers. The varied forms of prose and poetry, of journalism and the broadcast word, and of all the information available on the World Wide Web, are made much clearer by comparing the way the same story is told in different media.

Drama is a natural and central means of helping children extend their knowledge of the use of text, and the relationship between personality and story. Plays have the advantage of teaching children to enter the idea of a role: words read become words in action, a reversal of their normal sense of translation. This is, after all, the basis of reading: that children should see that the concept behind it is that there is a 'voice' attempting to emerge through the medium of print, that those words are not mere abstractions.

Plays are one way of involving children in the concept of reading for a purpose. We can also ask them to 'translate' one kind of writing into another, such as changing a story into a film, or into a play script. The same words can be used, but the concepts rethought. This can be a fairly simple matter of changing some of the instructions; it can become more complex as children get involved with the 'idea' of a film, an idea they do not find difficult to grasp since they see so many on television. Children can also be asked to retell a story from the point of view of one of its characters. This technique of helping children enter into different points of view can be used with news stories, or comics. While children are being asked to enter into a story or article imaginatively, they can also be asked to express their opinions about what they have read. This can take the form of recommendations to their friends, or notes written about a particular book so that others know what to expect. The many techniques that we can use to encourage children's expression of their opinions include asking them to advertise the books, or write a review for a particular journal, or write a 'blurb'. The easiest way to encourage their sense of how to do this is, in fact, through their sense of parody.

Chapter 20
The reading curriculum

The ability to read is essential in any part of the curriculum. Learning *how* to read has been a traditional part of the curriculum of the early years, and then discarded, as if, once the ability to decode messages fluently had been acquired, it was no longer a matter of importance. This policy has two damaging consequences. The first is that the 'skill' of reading (like mathematics) is depicted as something for its own sake, almost without a purpose beyond itself. The only point of reading, as a skill, is the consequence of being able to use it. This book concentrates on how difficulties can be overcome, but always stresses that the skill is not an end in itself, but something necessary for the whole of the curriculum, a fact we must not ignore.

The second consequence is that the real skills of reading, the engaging with texts in a variety of formulae, from archives to e-mail messages, is ignored. Learning how to interpret, and how to communicate, is the most important of educated acts, far beyond the ability to be tested on the accumulation of facts. The need for the ability to read literature and the need to be critical in reading have already been noted. The development of reading as a precise skill deserves further exploration.

The complaint of many teachers of sixth-form pupils, and lecturers in higher education about their pupils, is not that they tend to lack an adequate background in cultural references, but that they read in a superficial manner. There are many stages in learning, and in learning any new topic, at whatever point of our life, we need to go through all of them. The first stage of all is when we, in ignorance, feel we know all that we need to know. This is replaced by the realization that we know very little. The third stage is that moment when the excitement of learning new things suggests that every piece of information creates a wholly new theory of the case. The fourth stage makes us realize, as we see the dimensions of the subject, that it is very vast and very complex: we know too much to have any theory. The next stage is that of knowing that all we know about a subject fits, but we remain inarticulate about it since our knowledge is complex. The next to last stage (one often thought of as the final stage) is that of knowing the subject so well that we can talk lucidly and simply about it. In the end, of course, we not only go on learning other subjects, but realize the complexities of the relationship between one body of knowledge and another: that, perhaps, is true wisdom.

In the series of experiences that make up learning, the greatest worries are that people think they know the answers, and that they learn so superficially that they feel they have achieved mastery when this is far from being the case. The reason for this failure of learning lies not so much in the absence of adequate information as in the failure to read the information attentively. Almost every statement contains implications or needs some further gloss. To understand the limitations of *any* statement of fact it is necessary to read and understand the way it is presented as well as its ostensible meaning. This is not a particularly sophisticated task or specialized linguistic philosophy. The simple generalization may be adequate to those who do not know; to those who wish to know, the ambivalences of a statement will be apparent. The superficial reader always feels there is nothing more to say beyond the generalization. The close reader looks for more information.

It is easy to become lazy in reading. One form of laziness is to see reading as a way of finding particular information for which one is looking, like the relevant part of minutes or the conclusion of a textbook. Another form of laziness in reading is similarly a matter of looking for just enough clues to use in one's own fashion. The reading of headlines until 'something catches one's eye', or the romp through a detective story until one knows who has done it, are both forms of reading that are used for certain satisfactions. Sometimes they are used so much that it is very difficult to revert to reading anything demanding closer attention.

Fluent reading depends on the ability to respond to a text in a variety of different ways, and to find the appropriate type of response. One cannot make a basic distinction between skills and understanding. Real practice in fluent reading depends on confronting a variety of texts. Children can be encouraged to read anything, for they will learn about reading if they see the distinctly different uses to which it can be put.

There is no point in trying to keep children on one particular scheme, for that shows a mechanistic attitude to reading. However logical it seems to make children assiduously build up a 'controlled' vocabulary, this does not cohere with what we know about their styles of learning. Children derive benefit from their confrontation with script in a variety of different ways, whether the text is on a cornflake packet or in a newspaper, whether it is on hoardings or in novels, in computer games or sophisticated software. There are not just two types of text and types of response: reading for information or reading for imagination. This distinction is as misleading as that between thought and feeling. The truth is that every text makes a variety of demands, whether it intends to or not. We can, and should be able to, read in different ways, from scanning to careful scrutiny.

The more varied the types of material used to teach reading, the more aware children will be of the necessary variety of their responses. If children associate reading merely with a particular series of text-books, or link it to the habit of undergoing school, then they will never transfer their ability into their normal lives. It is by insistence upon certain stages and on narrow skills, on particular textbooks and on graded schemes, that we manage to keep some children slow readers: dogged with determination to do the 'right' thing, and never using their abilities to do the interesting one. We should use the materials that surround us, use children's curiosity and their awareness of their environment, to bring in the variety of texts that they will anyway be confronting. We will often be surprised at their ability to read what we imagine should be far beyond them. We should certainly help them perceive the variety of texts.

One distinction in the many different styles of reading is that of the speed with which a text is read. The average reading speed is about 240 words per minute; 170 words or less is very slow. A very fast reader will read about 550 words per minute, but at this stage the connection between the text and spoken language is almost entirely broken. The slowest readers 'listen' to what they read as if they were speaking it. The fastest readers depend on overcoming the usual connections of processes in reading, from visual to auditory, and from oral perception to understanding.

The connections of speed reading are made immediately between the visual recognition and understanding. Speed reading is a form of reading for information. It is a way of extracting the essentials from the text without taking in anything but the bare essentials. It is achieved by making a conscious effort to 'disconnect' the ears and tongue from the eyes, on the grounds that it is *hearing* the words that holds up our speed of reading, just as we read aloud far more slowly than we do silently to ourselves. Speed reading can be a useful device for some, but it ignores some of the essentials of a text. We miss the style, we ignore the mistakes, and while the essential points are extracted, it is only useful in those texts that have a few essential points to make. But many people become accustomed to this kind of reading. Those who take on large numbers of detective stories, or those who devour newspapers, learn to respond just to the essential pieces of information. They learn to glean only part of the text, and in the end can learn to treat all texts in the same way. Some novels might deserve speed reading; it is a dangerous device to impose on those demanding something more.

The real secret of advanced reading is close to the initial secret of learning how to read: the ability to concentrate with confidence. Nothing is more important than a close personal engagement with the text. It can be far easier to watch a film on television, but such an activity will make a difference to our ideas only if the film is looked at closely and critically. Once this critical faculty is engaged, reading becomes an art in its own right; and information is no longer seen as distinct from the way it is conveyed. Such attention is an important education in itself. Such critical attention is not just an acquired skill, but the art through which other skills are learnt.

It is because of the complex relationship between text and understanding that reading itself can become a part of the curriculum. Indeed, in the majority of universities in the United States all first-year undergraduates take courses in what is called 'freshman composition'; subtitled 'rhetoric'. These are, in fact, courses in reading. The idea of them is very good, but they are introduced about 10 years later in normal human development than they need to be. For this reason the lecturers spend much of their time complaining about teaching freshmen these courses, and see it as a type of punishment. The topics covered are very sensible: an analysis of how language is used; how to construct a clear argument; what kind of devices are used to persuade others; the sense of an audience; the sense of an author; what common faults emerge from hastily written prose. All these topics are basic to the development of reading in young children.

One of the major skills of reading lies in knowing which type is appropriate to the circumstances. We might not always have to concentrate if we are skimming through a detective story, but we remain very limited unless we can do so. Many children acquire the habit of reading just for information, and subsequently read only what is least demanding. They learn to extract a few items that they need and ignore the rest of the text, missing the way it is expressed. They start to learn how *not* to read a book through to the end.

Reading solely for topic work can have a deleterious effect. There was once a formula about how to read: 'SQ3R'. 'SQ3R' stood for 'survey, question, read, recite, review'. It was supposed to be a way of extracting the most information from a text, as if the text were a collection of facts. To survey is to flip through and see *beforehand* what is coming (a quick glance at the end of *King Lear*?). Used as a general device, 'SQ3R' implies that reading is a mechanical skill. Even the hastiest reading of a document to glean its main point is more subtle; reading not only contains all those processes at once, but implies the ability to discriminate between jargon and sense.

Reading and writing demand that we convey ideas in as exact a form as possible, quite unlike the scramble of self-corrections in speech. Written script makes what is said observable and analysable. It is only when the expression of new ideas becomes natural that any real learning takes place. No one can merely imbibe information. We need to make it our own by commentary and by use. No one can benefit by the mere passive reception of experience: it only becomes our own through active involvement. Children's responses to what they read deserve to be written. We cannot always prevent children looking at crime series on television, but we can help them become more critical, and more active, in their response. It is through writing, through becoming accustomed to expressing opinions, that children learn how to discriminate, and how to read properly.

One of the simplest ways of extending the ability to have ideas is by the encouragement of writing. It will lead to the art of understanding what a sentence means, to the ability to pick out the meaning of what is written, and the ability to understand basic logic. One way in which pupils can be helped to build up their own arguments is by asking them to number their points according to importance. Each major argument can have one number, each minor one a second number, as in the sequence 1.0, 1.1, 1.1.2, 2.0.

This device can be useful in helping pupils to develop awareness of the order of sentences that build up an argument. Pupils can also be asked to take a passage from a textbook or a newspaper and tabulate the argument in the same way, discovering very simply whether the text contains such structured logic. Even file cards – that specific way of imposing order on material – can be an interesting way of teaching pupils to store and organize ideas.

Readers are rarely conscious, as they scan a page, of any exact order of words, until they come across a typographical or grammatical error. Mistakes we notice quickly, like in the substitution of 'like' for 'as'. Basic syntax is fairly simple to learn: in fact young children are almost as soon aware of the significance of word order as of words, since our language depends so heavily on it. It is a useful exercise to give pupils a series of words in a jumbled order, out of which they construct a sentence that makes sense, provided that what they are given is a real challenge, and includes possible alternatives. Putting the words into the best order orally is itself useful, to encourage close attention, memory and the ability to judge how a sentence should be or can be formed. Pupils can be asked to make a logical argument by reconstructing a jumbled paragraph. The fact that there are different possibilities for the same collection of words means that children can see how many ways they can construct sentences with sensible meanings. There is not always only one 'correct' solution.

Fluent reading is an essential part of grammar; the two inevitably go together. Learning which word to use is akin to knowing what word to expect in reading. When pupils are asked to put the missing word into a sentence, a word like 'if', 'so' or 'because', they are learning how a sentence is constructed and learning the rudiments of argument. It is possible to teach sentence construction by the analysis of active and passive sentences, and it is especially useful to turn sentences from passive to active. Passages taken from books (like summaries of experiments) can be rewritten in a different form. A series of sentences, only some of which make grammatical sense, can teach not only the structure of sentences but the habit of close analysis while reading. We do not need to look far for examples of sentences that mean little: these are far easier to spot in other people's work than in our own. The ability to recognize mistakes of this kind is, however, an essential part of thoughtful reading.

Nearly all the means to develop reading as a skill involve a lot of writing. We develop our reading by having to write ourselves, whether we write long essays or shorter pieces: making notes, recording ideas, and expressing exactly what we wish to express. We are trying to give pupils material about which they have something to say. Not every child is going to be able to turn out something 'creative'. It is very difficult for most people to respond to a topic like 'sailing' or 'a day in the country' and think of anything interesting to say. Far more stimulating and personal is that writing which responds to given material. It is in the analysis of an article or an advertisement that the best creative work will emerge. There will be something to say and a reason for saying it. It is, in fact, as difficult and as good a training in creativity to write a description of something particular, as to try to invent a story or a poem.

By writing, pupils begin to understand how a text is put together, and how difficult it is to organize any material in a coherent, fluent way. It is useful to teach them how to construct an argument for a case. We can encourage them to write down all their ideas in a kind of 'free flow' to see what particular theme emerges. We can ask them to try to think of one small point that seems to them particularly important, once they have written down all they can think of. They can then be asked to summarize one incident that seems to them to stand as an example of all they have to say. By this means we will have approached the analysis of what is read by a different route. Reading is not a passive skill.

Conclusion

Every teacher, whether of a single child or a class of 30 children, hankers after a solution to the problem of reading that is simple, effective and fast. This is natural. The inability to read gets in the way of so many things, and often spoils the first experience of school. Without reading, a whole world of learning and understanding is closed. But parents and teachers can also find the teaching of reading frustrating, because it is so difficult to understand why some children of normal ability seem incapable of making sense of script. No explanation seems adequate. No amount of individual attention seems to make a difference. Teachers search for a solution for two reasons. One is out of sheer frustration at not knowing what the difficulty can be, the other is the natural human tendency to assume that there is a single systematic scheme which would, if used, enable all children to learn. However, there is no such scheme: the nature of human learning is too complex for that to be possible, and it does not fit a series of simple development stages. For all its learned simplification, the decoding of scripts is a complex process.

One day we will no doubt know so much about how people learn that it will be much simpler to close the vast divide between an individual's capacity and his or her achievements, between the potential in people and their common actions. Meanwhile, we still suffer from putting more faith in the idea of an imposed reading scheme than in the understanding of children's idiosyncratic development. Learning to read comes about through a combination of auditory, visual and linguistic skills, and the ability to image, associate and categorize. The capacity to read is a result of a combination of many things: the ability to concentrate, the sense of discrimination, the progress of language, and the curiosity in story that places children themselves in the context of the experiences around them. Learning to read is also a matter of knowing which clues in the coded world to ignore.

The process of reading is rarely placed in the context in which it actually takes place. Instead of understanding the richness of the surroundings and the complexity of the child's inner world, many approaches to reading show a tendency to impose a series of rules, as if there were a number of hurdles to overcome. Children then find that each hurdle is more like a barrier. Reading cannot be so narrowly systematized, or reduced to a series of tasks often uninteresting in themselves and cumulatively deadening. The context in which reading takes place, the world of perception, of language and the need to communicate, is what children use in learning to read. Just as they learn language by context, so they perceive the nature of reading. Our task is to enable this to take place, and we do this naturally from the moment that the child first communicates.

Many of the mistakes about reading arise because of the desire to make a scientific system out of what is an art. The desire to test a reading age in terms of vocabulary is itself a symptom of the respect paid to the measurable and the observable. A scheme that gives complicated details of sequences seems scientific and does enable reading to fit the characteristics of the education system as a whole: comparisons between children doing the same thing, and standard norms of achievement. The concept of 'reading readiness' can be interpreted as a particular 'stage' of development, dangerous to approach at the 'wrong' time. Readability suggests measurable distinctions of text in relation to the reader. Graded reading schemes suggest themselves as the mirrors of internal development.

The true principles of the development of learning are more complex and inward. The slow process of growing up includes repeated patterns of understanding and forgetfulness. Many of the tasks suggested in the book are appropriate to children at a particular age, but the principles are true of any stage. There are fundamental aspects of reading that need to be understood at whatever age the learner is. Each person brings his or her own unique awareness to bear on the nature of reading, whatever the age. Reading is therefore a process by which the individual's sense of understanding meets the way in which the social world chooses to communicate in a coded form. The teachers are those who have enough curiosity about the world, and enough sympathy with the individual, to bring the two successfully together.

By now it should be clear that there are consistent ground rules, which the many research studies reiterate, however complex is the personal experience of learning to read, and however damaging the external, political interference.

Any intervention, provided it is supportive, helps. Parents, teachers, other adults and other children can help the individual learn to read.

Knowledge of technical matters, such as phonemes and digraphs, is of great benefit: it clarifies the peculiar difficulties of decoding script. More important than the technical terms themselves, however, are the concepts.

A sense of purpose in reading is essential. Decoding script is not an end in itself, or something done for the purposes of academic attainment or fulfilling the demands of literacy, but has a greater outcome. The goal of reading should never be forgotten.

Having an early experience of reading in the widest sense, of pleasure in language and story, in visual and auditory refinement and in the demonstrations of texts, makes a crucial difference. Some children get this experience in the home, it is the task of teachers to give the experience to those that don't.

Using material that is interesting, and that demonstrates the utility of reading, is more important for slow readers than the simplicities of the text.

Interventions and instructions in how to overcome some of the difficulties of reading are more important and helpful than assessment for its own sake.

We need to acknowledge that reading combines two types of learning at once. It involves skills, analogous to driving a car, and it involves modifications to behaviour as a result of absorbed experience. It is this combination of precise and exact analogies and the wider aspects of reading that people find difficult. Both need addressing. If we understand how children learn to read, then we can do something to help.

Glossary

Allophones	The separate sounds that make up a phoneme. These do not correspond exactly with the letters of the alphabet. For example, the 'p' in 'spin' and the 'p' in 'pin' represent slightly different sounds, hence these are two different allophones.
Allographs	The different visual symbols for the same letter, ie. A and a.
Babbling	Babies' experiments with the sounds and tone of the language before they use words in the normal way.
Blends	The joining together of two sounds or two letters, as at the start of the word 'blend'.
Breakthrough to Literacy	A scheme for beginners that gives them letters and words from which they make up their own sentences.
Cloze procedure	A procedure in which a systematic number of words in a passage, for example one in five, are blanked over.
Colour coding	The use of colours to denote similarities of sounds despite differences in spelling. The final sounds in the words 'go' and 'dough' would therefore be marked by the same colour.

Diacritical marking	The use of extraneous marks to draw attention to peculiarities in orthography, as in the 'crossing out' of 'silent' letters: for example, write, right.
Digraphs	A combination of two letters that together make up one sound, as in 'th'.
Dyslexia	The inability to make much progress in reading owing to unusual physiological factors or environmental factors.
Fixations	The moments in reading when the eye is focused on a particular point (see also 'saccadic movements').
Graphemes	The term given to what makes a letter visually identified. The written equivalent of a *phoneme*.
Homonym	Words that sound alike but are spelt differently, eg plane/plain, pale/pail, pique/peak, or which have two meanings but are identical in both written and spoken forms, eg peer/peer, rail/rail (contrast with homographs, which are words where the two meanings are spelt alike but pronounced differently, eg tear/tear, read/read).
ita	Initial teaching alphabet. A system of changing the orthography by making consistent the relationship between the 44 spoken phonemes and their written equivalents, designed to be used up to the age of about eight, when transfer to traditional orthography (TO) takes place.
Key words	The concentration upon a limited set of words, to be learnt first as a basis for further reading development. (The same term has been used for words that are significant historically for a change of meaning, eg 'wisheit' from 1200 to 1300.)

Miscue analysis	The description of the mistakes that children make when reading, as an insight into the reading process, eg 'Readers develop sampling strategies to pick out only the most useful and necessary graphic clues' (Goodman, 1973, p.9).
Mnemonics	The use of visual associations as a device for remembering specific items.
Morphemes	The smallest unit of meaning contained within a word, eg the plural 's' changes the meaning of a word and is an individual morpheme.
Orthography	The spelling system of an alphabetic language.
Phoneme	The particular sounds that are recognized as having meaning in a language. English has 44 phonemes. Other languages have different phonemes: for example, 'b' and 'p' are distinct in English but not in Arabic, while 'p' is one phoneme in English but two in Bengali. In English the 'p' sounds in the words 'pin' and 'spin' are different allophones.
Phonics	The concentration on the isolated sounds that make up a word.
Proprioception	The sense that tells us where the mobile parts of our body are in relation to the rest.
Readability	The distinction between different texts in terms of the ease with which they can be read, depending either on the length of words and sentences or on the presentation, eg size of script.
Reading readiness	The necessary abilities that a child must possess, eg language, before being able to learn to read.

Reading schemes	Published material, usually graded, consisting mainly of books, designed for use in teaching children to read. Popular schemes include those published by Ladybird and teachers' instruction.
Saccadic movements	The movement of the eye, too quick for us to be aware of, as it travels in jumps from point to point in a text.
Semantics	The meaning of words.
Speed reading	A fast-reading technique that works by dissociating the text from the sounds the text implies.
Syntax	The structure of the language in terms of its grammatical features.
Syllables	The parts that can be heard to make up a word.

Notes and references

There is a huge amount of literature on reading, and there is a whole industry of research published in learned journals, particularly in the United States. Most of this is admirable and useful. It is also repetitive. There is a sense that we never quite fully understand how the mind works.

The problem with the empirical evidence on reading is it keeps reinventing itself, and despite that is rarely applied. Instead of the research, teachers receive a veritable industry of methods, of instructions, of advice, of the latest solution.

What follows are a few hints on further reading, and also an unobtrusive demonstration that the book is based on a great deal of evidence, on reading as well as practising!

Preface

For an account of the history of reading and the ambivalent social attitudes towards it see:

Altick, R (1957) *The English Common Reader*, Chicago University Press, Chicago

Many books point out the importance of seeing the art of reading in a holistic way, taking in as many parts as possible in order to understand the whole as an orchestra:

Adams, M (1990) *Beginning to Read: Thinking and learning about print*, MIT Press, Cambridge, Mass

Riley, J (1996) *The Teaching of Reading: The development of literacy in the early years*, Paul Chapman, London

In a survey that was used in the development of the Literacy Hour, David Wray observed and interviewed those English teachers who were considered the most successful. While they were clearly doing a marvellous job, they were not able to *describe* exactly what they did; they did not possess the nomenclature nowadays required of them. Does this diminish their teaching? In a number of studies on teacher education (for example that by Neville Bennett at Exeter) the teaching of reading remains a sore point. However many hours devoted to it, it seems that students subsequently tend to deny they were ever taught anything about reading.

Introduction

There are a number of texts that summarize what is understood about the process of learning, for example:

Cullingford, C (1999) *The Human Experience: The early years*, Ashgate, Aldershot

Goleman, D (1996) *Emotional Intelligence: Why it matters more than IQ*, Bloomsbury, London

Pinker, S (1995) *The Language Instinct: The new science of language and mind*, Penguin, London

Pinker, S (1998) *How the Mind Works*, Allen Lane, London

1 How children learn

In addition to those already mentioned are an array of readable texts:

Bruner, J (1994) *The Culture of Education*, Harvard University Press, Cambridge, Mass

Donaldson, M (1993) *Human Minds: An exploration*, Penguin, London

Gardner, H (1993) *Multiple Intelligence: The theory in practice*, Basic Books, New York

N Chomsky's book (1978) *Language and Mind*, Academic Press, London, was very influential as, in a quieter way, was J Dunn's (1987) *The Beginnings of Social Understanding*, Blackwell, Oxford

The young person's intellectual and emotional prowess is so recognized that there are even official reports accepting the evidence, although no one seems to do anything about it as a result (see *The Human Experience: The early years*). 'Conditioning' is particularly associated with B F Skinner's (1957) *Verbal Behaviour*, Prentice Hall, New Jersey, but the principles are still atavistically adhered to, as if behaviourism lives in practice. One should have been warned by William James's description of human instincts in *The Principles of Psychology* (1890). Piagetian research is nowadays discredited in many texts, or better still replaced, for example by the books of Kieran Egan, but again there is a tendency to believe that clear developmental 'stages' are a matter of common sense and observation.

2 The process of learning to read

There are many schemes, usually based in local authorities, which involve parents, with additional help for children who need it most, but these initiatives, which are too numerous to be listed individually, have never become a policy (but see notes to Chapter 16 for sample).

The research on reading has often been summed up, demonstrating the consistencies. See for example:

Croll, P and Hastings, N (eds) (1996) *Effective Primary Teaching: Research-based classroom strategies*, David Fulton, London

Owen, P and Pumfrey, P (eds) (1995) *Children Learning to Read: International concern*, Falmer, London

There are also a great many texts that concentrate on analysing the difficulties and coming up with one exclusive solution, such as:

McGuinness, N (1998) *Why Children Can't Read*, Penguin, London

Attacks on mechanical approaches to reading were at their height in the backlash to all the methods, like colour coding and ita, once fashionable. See:

Bettelheim, B and Zelan, K (1982) *On Learning to Read: The child's fascination with meaning*, Thames and Hudson, London

Smith, F (1971) *Understanding Reading: A psycholinguistic analysis of reading and learning to read*, Holt, Rinehart and Winston, New York

For 'miscue analysis' and the 'psycholinguistic guessing games' see:

Goodman, K (1982) *Language and Literacy*, Routledge and Kegan Paul, Boston

3 The skills of learning to read

There are many interesting examples of the peculiar difficulties of learning to read, alphabetical and motivational. Their connection to suggested actions can be narrow, or comprehensive, as in:

The Bullock Report (1975): *A Language for Life*, HMSO, London

Many of the explanations for the difficulties lie in the history of the development of the English language, like the great vowel shift. That, and the nature of language acquisition, can be topics of interest to pupils.

For those who wish to pursue the quote given, the reference is:

Mots d'heures: gousses, rames. The d'Antin manuscript, edited and annotated by Luis d'Antin van Rooten (1968) Angus and Robertson, London

Speed reading is not just a matter of glancing quickly over minutes but learning a technique of looking at print without making any connection with the *sounds* that are implied. It is the opposite end from mouthing every letter and says something about the combination of eye and ear involved in reading. The connection between language, talk, reasoning and reading is always important. See:

Mercer, N, Wegeruf, R and Dawes, L (1999) Children's talk and the development of reasoning in the classroom, *British Educational Research Journal*, 25(1), pp 95–111

4 Impediments to learning to read

I would like to think that in the future people will look back with astonishment at some of the educational policies and the focus on the wrong issues. The heyday of experiments with methods has been followed by central control, but significantly of literacy as an academic skill. The research literature on the way in which pressure to perform, to meet set targets, has the opposite effect to that intended, in also extensive.

Debates on reading are longstanding. See:

Chall, J and Sternlicht, J (1970) *Learning to Read: The great debate. An enquiry into the science, art and ideology of old and new methods of teaching children to read 1910–1965*, McGraw Hill, New York

Wray, D (1989) Reading: the new debate, *Reading*, **23**(1), pp 2–8

The perceived success of intervention programmes is different from their actual success. See:

Somerville, D and Leach, D (1988) Direct or indirect instruction? An evaluation of three types of intervention programmes for assisting students with specific reading difficulties, *Educational Research*, **30**(1), pp 46–53

This is partly because of the complexity of reading; there are many different ways of learning to read. See:

Ehri, L (1995) The emergence of word reading in beginning reading, in *Children Learning to Read: International concern*, ed P Owen and P Pumphrey, pp 9–31, Falmer, London

5 Auditory perception

There is a growing literature on the detection of sound, connected to timbre and of interest to musicians, but it also has a direct application to the understanding of phonemes. The ground has been well established for some time. See for example:

McPherson, D and Thatcher, J (1977) *Instrumentation in the Hearing Sciences*, Grune and Stratton, New York

Singh, S and Singh, K (1976) *Phonetics: Principles and practice*, University Park Press, Baltimore

The importance of rhyme is constantly reiterated. See:

Bryant, P and Bradley, L (1985) *Children's Reading Problems: Psychology and education*, Blackwell, Oxford

Letter sounds are significant in themselves. See:

Treiman, R, Tincoff, R, Rodriguez, K, Monzaki, A and Francis, D (1998) The foundations of literacy: learning the sounds of letters, *Child Development*, **69**(6), pp 1524–40

Understanding phonology clearly helps reading. See:

Goswani, U and Bryant, P (1990) *Phonological Skills and Learning to Read*, Lawrence Erlbaum, London

Hatcher, P, Hulme, C and Ellis, A (1995) Ameliorating early reading failure by integrating the teaching of reading and phonological skills: the phonological linkage hypothesis, *Child Development*, **65**(1), pp 41–57

6 Visual perception

There are a number of readable texts on seeing, including:

Gregory, R (1966) *The Intelligent Eye*, Weidenfeld, London

Gregory, R (1970) *Eye and Brain*, Weidenfeld, London

For the 'Sapir-Whorf' hypothesis, that language shapes thought, see:

Whorf, P (1956) *Language, Thought and Reality*, MIT Press, Cambridge, Mass

See also Pinker (op cit) and books on memory such as:

Underwood, G (1926) *Attention and Memory*, Pergamon, Oxford

Bartlett, F S (1932) *Remembering: A study in experimental and social psychology*, Cambridge University Press, Cambridge – is still fresh

7 Psychomotor skills

This is a field in which Piagetian research still has something to offer, for example:

Furth, H and Wachs, H (1974) *Thinking Goes to School*, Oxford University Press, Oxford

William James (op cit) is always worth reading. The attention given to the importance of young children's physical activity – constructive play – is quite right; they want to create things, and not just watch them.

8 Attitudes to reading

There has been a great deal of valuable research on the importance of dialogue between adults and pre-school children, stressing the need for intellectual relationships, such as:

Cullingford, C (1999) *The Causes of Exclusion*, Kogan Page, London

Wells, G (1985) *Language Development in the Pre-School Years*, Cambridge University Press, Cambridge

Richman, N, Stevenson, J and Graham, P (1982) *Pre-School to School: A behavioural study*, Academic Press, London

Reading activity at home helps significantly, regardless of socio-economic circumstances. See:

Munn, P (1995) What do Children know about reading before they go to school?, in *Children Learning to Read: International concern*, ed. P Owen and P Pumphrey, pp 104–14, Falmer, London

Rowe, K (1991) The influence of reading activity at home or students' attitudes towards reading, *British Journal of Educational Psychology*, **61**(1), pp 19–35

The importance of early literacy has long been established, for example in:

Lunzer, F and Gardner, K (1979) *The Effective Use of Reading*, Heinemann, London

Stories and fairy tales are a matter of constant fascination. See, for example:

Bettelheim, B (1976) *The Uses of Enchantment*, Thames Hudson, London

Zipes, J (1993) *Fairy Tales and the Art of Subversion*, Heinemann, London

Parents' involvement, a delight in stories, and the association of reading with pleasure (not always achieved in school) are all vital ingredients often demonstrated in the journals. There are so many references they stop me in my tracks. Parents should never be afraid to give instructions. See:

Burns, J and Collins, M (1987) Parents' perceptions of factors affecting the reading development of intellectually superior accelerated readers and non-readers, *Reading Research and Instruction*, **26**(4), pp 239–46

See also Cullingford, C (1998) *Children's Literature and Its Effects*, Cassell, London

9 Helping children to read

Teachers, as well as parents, are often studied for the ways they can help. See:

Greenhough, P and Hughes, M (1998) Parents' and teachers' interventions in children's reading, *British Educational Research Journal*, **24**(4), pp 383–98

Lovett, M, Borden, S, Lacerenza, L and Fritzers, J (2000) Components of effective remediation for developmental reading disabilities: combining phonological and strategy-based instruction to improve outcomes, *Journal of Educational Psychology*, **92**(2), pp 263–83

Opie, S (1995) Effective teaching of reading: a study of personal qualities and teaching approaches in a group of successful teachers, *Educational Psychology in Practice*, **11**(2), pp 3–7

Somerville, D and Leach, D (1988) Direct or indirect instruction? An evaluation of three types of intervention programme for assisting students with specific reading difficulties, *Educational Research*, **30**(1), pp 46–53

Wade, B and Dewhirst, W (1983) Reading comprehension revisited, *Educational Research*, **25**(3), pp 171–76

11 Letters and letter blends

Again, there are many papers on the distinct skills associated with phonology, such as:

Ball, E and Blackman, B (1991) Does phoneme awareness training in kindergarten make a difference in early world recognition and developmental spelling? *Reading Research Quarterly*, **26**(1), pp 49–66

Goswani, U and Bryant, P (1990) *Phonological Skills and Learning to Read*, Lawrence Erlbaum, London

Hatcher, P, Hulme, C and Ellis, A (1995) Ameliorating early reading failure by integrating the teaching of reading and phonological skills: the phonological linkage hypothesis, *Child Development*, **65**(1), pp 41–57

Treiman, R, Tincoff, R, Rodriguez, K, Monzaki, A and Frances, D (1998) The foundations of literacy: learning the sounds of letters, *Child Development*, **69**(6), pp 1524–40

12 Word building

It is virtually impossible to separate phonics, and phonology from the ways in which words are constructed. See:

Johnstone, R, Connelly, V and Watson, J (1995) Some effects of phonic teaching on early reading development, in *Children Learning to Read: International concern*, ed P Owen and P Pumphrey, pp 32–42, Falmer, London

Learning how to spell is also something that comes early, taught as well as caught. See:

Graham, S (2000) Should the natural learning approach replace spelling instruction? *Journal of Educational Psychology*, **92**(2), pp 235–47

13 Reading for meaning

A number of texts convey the excitement in children's learning of language and its connections with texts, such as:

Miller, G (1977) *Spontaneous Apprentices: Children and language*, Seabury Press, New York

The very sharing of a text makes a crucial difference. See:

Toomey, D (1993) Parents learning how children read: a review. Rethinking the lessons of the Haringey project, *Educational Research*, **35**(3), pp 223–36

16 Particular problems in learning to read

Some examples of intervention programmes are:

- Basic Skills Agency – Family Literacy Programmes
- Book Trust – Bookstart Project
- Peers Early Education Partnership
- York University scheme in Cumbria

- Programme on Phonic Awareness training (Pembrokeshire)
- Literacy Initiatives for teachers (Westminster LEA)
- Success for all (Nottinghamshire)
- First Steps (Tameside and Wiltshire)
- 'THRASS': Teaching handwriting, reading and spelling skills (Manchester and Cheshire)
- Paired Reading and Fastlane (Kirklees)
- Reading recovery (Surrey and New Zealand)

And the ultimate example: Literacy Hour.

Dyslexia is a particular problem that has had a number of explanations and interventions (like Irlen lenses: special glasses). See:

Filippaton, D and Pumfrey, P (1996) Pictures, titles, reading accuracy and reading comprehension: a research review, *Educational Research*, **38**(3), pp 259–91

Livingstone, M and Galaburda, A (1990) *Proceedings of the National Academy of Sciences, USA*

Lowenstein, L (19) Dyslexia – a review of literature, *Education Today*, **46**(3), pp 25–32

Quin, V and Macauslan, A (1991) *Dyslexia: What parents ought to know*, Penguin, Harmondsworth

Shute, R (1991) Treating dyslexia with tinted lenses: a review of the evidence, *Research in Education*, **46**, pp 39–48

18 The uses of literacy

A lot of advice is available on the books that appeal to children, beyond Harry Potter. Children have firm views of their own tastes. See:

Cullingford, C (1998) *Children's Literature and its Effects*, Cassell, London

Reading critically is to be encouraged; indeed so is thinking rather than imbibing facts. See:

Quinn, V (1997) *Critical Thinking in Young Minds*, David Fulton, London

Index

advertisements 143, 178, 179–80, 211
alphabet 36, 91, *91*, 97, 160
assessment 170–74
  diagnosis 170, 171–72
  individual needs 172, 173
  learning styles, knowledge of 171
  reading skills, understanding of 171
  tests/testing 170–71, 173
associations, learning through 14
auditory perception 41–50
  babbling 48
  conversations between children 50
  describing objects/pictures 49
  familiar phrases 47
  further reading 216–17
  glottal stop 43
  language development 48
  listening skills 42–43, 44–45, 48
  Morse code 46
  music, use of 45
  parents, involvement of 41, 48

parodies/role-playing 50
phonemes/phonology 43, 44
pronunciation, differences in 43
reading, conditions for 41–42
rhyme(s) 46, 47
significance of speech 44
sounds, distinguishing 43–44
syllables, sense of 46
word games/jingles 46, 47
words, construction of 47–48

babies 16, 51, 53, 54, 55, 60, 65
  see also psychomotor skills
  babbling 48, 49, 207
books, the use of 148–57
  children helping each other 156
  cloze procedure 153
  drama, use of 156–57
  literacy hours 151, 154–56 *see also* intervention programmes
  parent/teacher enthusiasm, value of 151
  parody 157
  readability 152–54
  reading for pleasure 149–50, 151